9 NOVEMBER 1990 - 6 JANUARY 1991

Possible Worlds

S C U L P T U R E F R O M E U R O P E

Institute of Contemporary Arts, London

Serpentine Gallery, London

Miroslaw Balka

Stephan Balkenhol

Jean-Marc Bustamante

Asta Gröting

Juan Muñoz

Thomas Schütte

Franz West

Preface

Possible Worlds marks the first collaboration between the ICA and the Serpentine Gallery. The starting point for the exhibition was a desire to redress the balance in Britain between the vigorous presentation of British sculpture over the past decade on the one hand, and on the other, the comparative lack of awareness or direct knowledge of parallel developments elsewhere in Europe.

Possible Worlds is not constituted as a review or survey. It highlights specific positions and examines the interrelation of their theoretical and formal concerns. The installations in both galleries are determined by this network of correspondences. It seemed important to present the work of each artist within a self-contained, discrete space, rather than producing a visual and conceptual mixture of their different practices. The installation therefore follows the spatial conditions of each gallery: the work of Jean-Marc Bustamante, Juan Muñoz and Franz West can be seen in the three spaces at the ICA, that of Miroslaw Balka, Stephan Balkenhol, Asta Gröting and Thomas Schütte in the four spaces of the Serpentine Gallery.

In making this exhibition possible we would like to thank The Stanley Thomas Johnson Foundation (Switzerland), The Henry Moore Foundation, The Arts Council International Initiatives Fund, Visiting Arts, The British Council, The Goethe Institut, The Association Française d'Action Artistique, and the Polish, Austrian and Spanish Ministries of Culture for their generous financial support. We are also grateful to all the public and private lenders who have generously allowed works to be included in *Possible Worlds.*

We have worked closely with Miroslaw Balka, Stephan Balkenhol, Jean-Marc Bustamante, Asta Gröting, Juan Muñoz, Thomas Schütte, and Franz West, and are indebted to them for their unfailing enthusiasm and commitment.

IB, JL, AS
London, October 1990

Objects of Experience
Experience of Objects

The sculptural revolution of the 1960s has provided both a discipline and a language for a subsequent generation of artists in Europe. The urgent search for radical new sculptural forms which manifested itself from 1962 onwards, and was later categorised as Minimalism, Pop and Conceptual Art and Arte Povera, produced a greatly increased sculptural vocabulary as well as a number of specific languages constructed from it. The vernacular and the commonplace, the assertion of the physical (as opposed to the metaphysical) and the serial (as opposed to the singular) combined with a merging of the distinction between abstraction and representation were recurrent concerns, particularly in the United States[1]. However, though the questioning of authorship was implicit in much of this work, it did not engender the reduction of individual artistic positions to generalities. One has only to think of the distinct achievements of Andre, Hesse, Judd, Nauman and Oldenburg to communicate this sense of individual identity within collective concerns.

As attention in the 1980s shifted from a predilection for the "Hot" to a preference for the "Cool" (to repeat Marshal McLuhan's distinction between Abstract Expressionism and Minimalism), a proclivity for the repackaging and reformulating of the languages established in the 1960s was almost inevitable. Minimalism in particular has been vulnerable to such processes, its language adopted and then inflected with a personal accent, or intonation, or given a conspicuously discrete signature. As a language, it has been abused and used in equal measure.

What distinguishes the artists in this exhibition is precisely that their indebtedness (which in any case varies considerably from artist to artist and is by no means limited to this particular moment in the history of sculpture) is embedded within the body of their work and not displayed as a legitimating sign. It is the difference between a position and a posture. And whereas the cynical recycling of the image of these languages remains doomed within an increasingly rarefied discourse, an assertion of possibility, albeit one coloured by scepticism, is implicit in the work of the generation in Europe to whom this exhibition is devoted (including sculptors in Britain who do not constitute a part of this exhibition). Their sculptural languages are neither systematic nor closed; the rigour of the work is not dependent on the reductiveness of the system.

The rapid invention of new forms for sculpture and the equally rapid extension of what could constitute sculpture (with the eventual dematerialisation of the object) has fuelled expectations of the need for a constant formal radicalism. But as Jeff Wall has commented both on Minimalism and Arte Povera, "the resulting new forms, rooted in an erudite ideology of radical openness, have begun to display their own hardened and sanctified surfaces, their own museal pomp, their own monumental closure against the everyday world in the glamour of their triumph."[2] In response, the propositions of the artists in this exhibition constitute an opening of sculptural possibilities without the radicality of inventing new languages or creating radically new forms. At the same time, they avoid swinging too violently towards the personal. They seek no recourse in the consolations of historicism, mythology or what the German writer Christa Wolf called "unfettered subjectivism".

So, although the sculptural languages of the 1960s provide both a discipline and a measure for these artists, their inventory is nonetheless drawn from the immediate, recognisable and inhabited everyday world. And although this inventory includes those industrial and mechanical processes and the characteristics of seamlessness and seriality which determined the closed forms of Judd and Andre, these forms have been fractured and fragmented.

In the fissures which have appeared within the monolithic forms, in the interstices, the specifics of culture and experience have been reinstated. A sculpture by Jean-Marc Bustamante, *Bac à Sable*, is a concrete and wood rectangle enclosing a pit of sand; the sand not only softens the hard edged aesthetic of the box, but also suggests a place of play and childhood memory. Similarly, the long lines of desks in a classroom in one of his *Lumières*, which run away from the viewer towards the great black square of the blackboard, are disrupted by one or two pupils who disrupt the linear and serial arrangement. Artists too, fidget under this evocation of Malevich's heroic proposal, unable to project grand visions into an imaginary future. They have no desire to propose again those prescriptive utopian causes of the 1920s whose reverberations may finally have been said to have exhausted themselves fifty years later, and whose death-throes have been enacted in primarily didactic terms.

But rather than mourning the failure of the modernist project, as have so many artists of the last decade, the attitude of these artists is more pragmatic. They do not attempt to extract themselves either from their historical condition (or indeed from their regional culture), but nor do they seek to exploit or parade this condition, as did painters in the 1980s. They offer propositions with which to negotiate the business of everyday life, sometimes with the unfettered wisdom of the child. The work is situated in the Here and Now of existence and survival. The vegetables and fruits in Thomas Schütte's sculptures and drawings are not primarily a reference to popular culture, or vernacular forms, but establish themselves as symbols of sustenance and nourishment. The sculptural forms in *Possible Worlds* - fruit, sandpit, cupboard, chair, stomach and bed - are fundamental to existence. They refer to human activities, to eating, digesting, sitting, storing and sleeping and to the memory of them. They propose a world of direct experience, of relationships which are immediate as much as mediated, and the value of fundamental necessities.

Dick Hebdige has appropriately suggested that "it is no longer a question of pushing corks out of bottles (the bottle representing the world of appearances, of disorder, of the inauthentic), but of coming to terms with the fact of our immersion, with the fact that we are held tight in the nets of these traditions and languages which constitute and place us and which, even as we struggle against them determine the angles of our attempted lines of flight".[3] This condition of immersion and participation in culture was of course the motivating factor of Pop Art and its obsession with conspicuous patterns of, and objects for, consumption. Although the obsession has been renewed in some recent American sculpture, a difference with a European attitude needs to be delineated. The sculpture of Koons and Steinbach, for example, participates in a fetishistic consumer aesthetic which tends to reinforce the alienated position of the spectator. The object, awaiting its transformation from fetish to consumption, is emblematic of the alienation precisely to the extent that it remains unconsumed, unexploited, unused. By contrast, the American preoccupation with surface and the ready-made, has been displaced by the used and the handmade. Indeed, in one of Franz West's sculptures, its ready-made core, a bottle, has been encased in manually applied papier maché. The found object is covered up by the artist to correspond to some inner picture, some inescapable rightness which will trigger collective recognition. Miroslaw Balka painstakingly constructs his own bed, making it simultaneously generic and unique. This elaboration of labour, here tentative and innocently clumsy, is taken into the realm of polished craftsmanship in the exquisite wooden inlays of Juan Muñoz's floor or Asta Gröting's enormous glass digestive systems. Reconstituted within the space of the exhibition, these are not so much symbols of a societal condition as objects of experience.

An insistence on the materiality of the object, on the special way it is made, shifts it from the allegoric to the poetic. More than just a critique either of consumption, of the predigested sameness of the mass produced; or of the suicide of art on the altar of design, these artists rescue art from 'enslavement to the washing machine' (as the Bauhaus aesthetic was denounced by the Situationists some twenty years before). It was more than the merely kitsch possibilities offered by a mass produced madonna that motivated Katharina Fritsch to use this devalued symbol. A key figure in suggesting a new agenda, Fritsch painted her madonnas a vivid lemon yellow to release an aura of spirituality from this banal figure. The ubiquitous is reinvested with a sense of the singular; and the everyday is heightened or shifted sideways to release its poetic and contemplative potential.

These propositions exist somewhere between the tradition of the radically closed, hard, autonomous object typified by Judd and the equivalent tradition of the radically fragmented form reconstituted in installation, as exemplified by Kounellis. Their status delineates a difference both from radical closure and fragmentary openness. If a minimal object, or series of objects stand for themselves, an Arte Povera object stands as a symbol in a cultural situation. The objects in *Possible Worlds* adhere to neither position with any ideological certitude. The exactness with which each idea is materialised into form, into its provisional totality, does not lead to inevitable seamlessness. The idea is embodied in the work as a precise manifestation of an intuitive process, and control is neither sacrificed nor reified. They share an attention to the intrinsic quality of materials - to papier maché, brick, glass, wood, ceramics, silicon without strictly adhering to a "truth to materials" credo.

Further, the configuration, or ensemble of objects in the space of the exhibition is similarly neither systematic nor fragmentary. The objects here have a life of their own, yet each one relates to, and is rendered more complex, by its relation to others. These are forms which converse with one another, across dramatic shifts in scale, pictorial languages, and artistic discipline; the drawings of Muñoz, the watercolours and banners of Schütte and the photographic pictures or *tableaux* of Bustamante are necessary constituents of their sculptural places. Each item in the assembly relates dynamically to the whole, whilst retaining its autonomy.

How these objects are experienced is of equal importance. It has been a commonplace that Minimalism, for all its reductiveness and rejection of narrative, embodied an implicitly theatrical relationship. The arrangements of objects on wall or floor necessitated the active relationship of the viewer not simply to the objects themselves, as in the conventional circling of a three-dimensional form, but to the space in which they were presented. The theatrical relationship revolves around a concept of separation between viewer and viewed even in the least hierarchical forms of theatre. Writing about Walter de Maria's *The 5 Continent Sculpture* presented at the Staatsgalerie in Stuttgart in 1988, Lars Nittve noted that the separation between the viewer and the work could be understood as an expression of the theatrical.[4] Similarly, Paul Virilio observed of Mucha's installations "Despite appearances, his work is objective theatre, the acts progressing in silence in a mise-en-scène of momentary stasis."[5]

This theatrical relationship of viewer to object permeates the spaces of *Possible Worlds*. The play and the players, the artist and the objects invite participation of the viewer. Yet at the same time the work insists on maintaining a distance. Bustamante's works both desire and repel the audience who are led, like Cocteau's rubber-gloved Orphée, into the boundless world beyond the mirror, yet bruise their shins on the metal frame that prevents entry. Franz West invites the spectator to try on his *Passtück* or "fitted pieces" but they make the viewer adopt such literally absurd, contorted positions that the temptation is better resisted. Distance is a necessary device in determining the autonomy of the sculpture as well as in resisting the reduction of the work into immediate personal narratives.

The immersion described by Hebdige is counterbalanced by the authority of the objects and the particular way in which they are installed. The territory delineated by *Possible Worlds* is therefore a space which activates the dialectical relationship of fragment and whole without aspiring to a resolution. Within this space indeed, a host of other dialectical relations are established: between infinity and delineation, separation and contact, apprehension and desire. This space reaffirms the possibility of experiencing art which resists didacticism or absorption. It uses distance neither to aggrandise the artist nor exclude the viewer. Of this relationship Carolyn Christov-Bakargiev commented "...there seems to be the need to reformulate a new subjectivity, and there comes to be a questioning of the more cynical postmodern thought, the need for at least an image of a society no longer alienated from labour and direct contact with 'things'."[6] It can be argued that the dialectical intervals created by these artists evoke a sense of real value in the teeth of commodification, of respite without escape, of aura without transcendence.

Part of that process of affirmation expresses itself in a concern with the human body, in its incorporation and its representation. In discussing the sculpture of the 1970s and 1980s, Jeff Wall has noted that "The emphasis... on the experience of objects, whether fragmented or condensed, tends towards a polarised and static subject-object relationship. In this, the object no matter how densely it is installed in a historical or semantic context, stands opposed to the body of the spectator as a theoretical thing, a thing which is at once sharply distinct from the body and which replaces it as the focal point of culture. This experience of the replacement of the body by things is an experience of essential alienation."[7] The creation of "objects of experience", of objects which communicate a history of use-value rather than of exchange-value may indicate a temporary release from, or resistance to, the condition of alienation. This does not indicate any proposition of an improvement nor any utopian subtext - an emphasis on progress is not a primary structure on which these artists can build (Schütte's model, with its slogan to eat, live, work could not make this more clear). It indicates that it is only on the basis of relative things and complex relations that any picture of existence can be made.

The human figure in sculpture has had to endure, more than any other form, the impositions of ideologies whose totalitarianism eliminated any space for the recognition of complexity and difference. The statuary and monuments of absolutist regimes from German and Italian Fascism in the 1930s to post-war Stalinism and its affiliates as well as recent converts to the cause of colossal statuary such as Saddam Hussein (in Baghdad, an enormous avenue is bridged by two vast bronze arms cast directly from the President's body) used the human figure as a vehicle to impose a certain and irrefutable value-system. Alternatively Columbian drug barons erect monuments to rock and roll heroes like John Lennon or Jimi Hendrix in remote peasant villages. That the body is implicated, and the figure incorporated, alongside a repertory of other recognisable things in this exhibition, may suggest the reopening of a possibility for the figure beyond the debasements of ideology and kitsch alike.

Juan Muñoz foregrounds figures whose position is socially marginal - dwarves, puppets, ballerinas - and locates them somewhere between pathos and the heroic. Such figures exist to perform and to be viewed. They are demarcated by social conventions as different, and outside, yet they exist. More directly Stephan Balkenhol reoccupies the territory scorched by totalitarianism. His figures deny monumentality, embrace ordinariness. They stand alone, yet an attempt to seize their individuality as a photograph might attempt to capture it, is always fated to be frustrated. Their individuality is always reclaimed by the crowd. Standing within this dialectical relationship, Balkenhol's figures both recognise the essentially alienated condition of modern humanity, and stand against it. The concern to picture directly the body as neither heroic, shamanistic, corporate, folkloric or politic, is part of a wish to reconnect with the real. They cannot offer a consummation of this desire, but they recognise that it exists.

In their scepticism and in their openness, these sculptors delineate a territory which is provisional, irreducible to certainties or systems. These are artists who recognise the fragmentary and contingent nature of experience much as Baudelaire demanded of his "Painter of Modern Life" almost one hundred and fifty years ago. It is neither possible nor advisable to collapse these artists into a group or movement, just as it is difficult to define what makes them European. In rejecting the ideology of newness, they do not suggest that images and objects are used up. They do not reject the past, but reinvest it with a contemporary and socio-political dimension. They do not deny the present, but draw on collective memory, fundamental processes, everyday activities, rituals and surroundings. They are not preoccupied with loss, nor do they propose unquestioning figures of hope. Resisting the temptation of millennial foreclosure they propose possible worlds of complexity and contradiction in the here and now.

Iwona Blazwick
James Lingwood
Andrea Schlieker

FOOTNOTES
1 For a more detailed schedule of the constituent aspects of Minimalism, see Michael Craig-Martin, *The Art of Context*, in *Minimalism*, Tate Gallery Liverpool, 1989, p.6
2 Jeff Wall, *Stephan Balkenhol*, Kunsthalle Basel, 1988
3 Dick Hebdige, *The Concept, Swimming Underwater*, Imagination Building, 1990, referring to Gianni Vattimo, Cultural Studies, Vol 2, No.I, 1988
4 Lars Nittve in *Walter de Maria, Two Very Large Presentations*, Moderna Museet, Stockholm,1989, pp.106-107
5 Paul Virilio, *Reinhard Mucha*, Centre Georges Pompidou, Paris, 1986, translated into English in Parachute, December 1986-February 1987, p.6
6 Carolyn Christov-Bakargiev, *Something Nowhere*, Flash Art, May/June 1988
7 Jeff Wall, ibid

2 x 24 x 24 x 8 in
1 x 2 x 24 x 8 in 1990
wood, marble

Miroslaw Balka

Why do you use such humble, second-hand materials?

I choose them because they carry a history which I connect with when I touch them. It is like kissing the hand of history. My touch represents the contemporary.

So the radical strategies of Arte Povera - of challenging notions of value by using degraded materials - do not apply? You choose them because they have a narrative function?

For me the history of materials is more important than the history of art. I don't make any connection with Arte Povera, but rather base my decisions on my own private experience. These are the materials I encounter in my studio, they constitute my personal landscape.

It seems that you are not so much interested in inventing new forms, as in arranging objects, assembling things and exploring the relationship between them?

Yes, I'm not looking for new forms. For me the problem of art is not one of imagination, or of the invention of the new. It is rather a way of abstracting that which is well known, the familiar and the useful. For example, the bed. It is important for me to make it in the traditional way; I don't want to reinvent the bed, but I would like to make this bed both universal and singular.

Why don't you find a ready made bed?

It gives me great pleasure to make it myself. I'm also a purist, I don't like outside interventions. For example, I can spend hours deciding in which way I should cut a plank. For me it is a very important decision. I am looking for this kind of energy hidden in simple decisions. By making a conscious decision I put my signature on the object.

The objects you make look functional, but they are not. The bed is too narrow, the bookshelf is empty.

These things look like they can be used but they are also abstractions. And in reality they are useful. The bed is where we spend at least a third of our lives, it's where we dream, where we make love, it's deeply private. But at the same time as soon as it's on public display it can remind one of a hospital or prison bed, a surgery table, something from an external situation. So there is a duality between private and public.

The installation you made in Venice was not an arrangement of discrete objects, but very powerfully suggested a room, a private space.

It is the problem of a privacy which can be public. It's also touching a sameness of experience, some people spend their whole lives in the same home, the same room, and looking through the same window to the space of dreams outside. It is like a life but it's made by me, it's based on situations of my own experience.

Do you see the austerity of this place you have created as being innocent of adornment, simple and not yet loaded with objects of comfort etc. Or is it pared down, reduced to something hard and ascetic?

For years I lived in a very restricted personal environment; now I have a situation when I can see an object in some order, so when I put the knife on the table, I know that this knife must be arranged in this way. Maybe now is the time to clean everything up and to define what are the real, meaningful objects. My choices are made by a sort of domestic history, how long I spend close to the table, how many times I step across the doorstep.

Do these things have only an autobiographical function or do you intend that they should have a broader meaning?

Of course if I as an artist display my private experience it takes on broader meaning. The problem for me is to establish a relationship with the viewer, to give something they can recognise.

Do you see your work as being a metaphor for a state of absence or failure? Does the empty bookshelf represent a failure of language or communication?

Deeper meanings come out of this personal history. But I don't like to start my work from the dictionary as some artists seem to do, of taking meaning and then making an object to illustrate it. I do it the other way round. At first I make a table and then you can look for an explanation in the symbols dictionary. I make decisions based on very simple, fundamental things. The titles of my sculptures are their measurements. I recently changed from metric to feet and inches, discovering at the same time that my foot measures exactly one foot. A new work - a dry aqueduct - measures exactly six feet of salt. It's a great pleasure when you can touch something so basic.

Why in the midst of all these very poor, austere materials, did you include alabaster?

Partly it was inspired by my grandfather and father's work as monument/tombstone masons. It's also about the different feeling of rotten planks with smooth alabaster. With the Venice installation, there is a tension between the attraction of the bed, and the unpleasantness of touching it. There is an electric pillow but it's hard. When I use marble it's like the stone in the plum. The fruit may be rotten but the stone is smooth and fresh and suggests new life. You can put it in the earth and grow something new. Including a material used for tombstones also raises the question of whether this piece is a grave. The alabaster also provided a surface on which to lay the pine needles. It was like selecting someone from the crowd, as soon as you isolate even a tiny element like that out of a mass where everything looks the same it takes on a special importance. The needles are in a sense nostalgic because they are the last remnants of the Christmas tree, the needles it has dropped by the end of the holiday. But they're also like the stone in the fruit. Small, but enduring, the life of the tree. A never ending story, the circle of life and death.

An element of this installation which seemed very important was an angled 'shelf' or sill on the floor behind which you had neatly swept away the dust. It suggested the retention of human dignity even in the most impoverished of circumstances.

This piece defined the border of the installation. And the ashes are those from the fire that keeps me warm in the studio mixed with the dirt on the floor in Venice. It is a sort of symbolic sweeping. I found a small piece of paper from a Chinese restaurant in the dust I was sweeping - the 'fortune' from a Chinese cookie. It's there under the sill, a diamond in the ashes.

Perhaps the most compelling elements in your work however, are those more abstract ones, such as your wall pieces. They're both two and three dimensional. They look functional but defy definition.

For me they are like unfinished or abstract sentences. Certainly not European sentences; more like the Japanese 'Haiku' poems. '... and the bird...' There is no beginning and no end. The bed on the other hand suggests logical progressions - 'This is a bed on which there is an electric pillow'; and then -'the bed sits on a concrete floor which is cold; the electric pillow is giving out heat' and so on. These other pieces cannot be explained in a useful way which I like very much.

There is a tremendous sense of poignancy about the work. It also looks like a vision from the past, a sort of concrete memory. Is it about mourning in some way?

Like a Tarkowski film! Well there is a kind of nostalgia you have in your blood. For me there is no border between my life and my art, so it is difficult to say where life finishes and the art begins. I think the reason Beuys' work is so powerful is because it flows from him, it is autobiographical.

Your work shares many formal similarities with Beuys. Was he an influence?

It is difficult to define any actual influence as I only recently had information about Beuys. But you could say my branch comes from the same tree. It's a tree which does not forget about its roots which can be more important than the branches. Beuys showed how important autobiography is for the artist. I feel the same. For years in Poland everything was collectivised, everything belonged to the nation. So I turned inwards to my own personal situation. But my life experience is different to Beuys, I grew up in a provincial situation and I use this situation. I am not the hero.

One of the foremost proponents of the antihero - the tramp, the derelict is Samuel Beckett, an author whose work you are often associated with.

His books were a really important part of my education, of growing up. I felt something similar in Beckett, that when I did my works they were almost like sentences from his books; his asceticism, his description of the very private. But even before Beckett, there was Joyce, especially his *Portrait of the Artist as a Young Man*.

In the past you have used religious titles, or made allusions to religious figures such as Saint Wojciech. In a way it is surprising because it presumes a shared orthodoxy in a country where religion had been suppressed.

We were brought up with the church as part of our lives. During martial law many Polish artists even exhibited in churches. You could describe my early works as Catholic in a sense; but later I moved to the simplicity of Protestantism. I was interested in exploring notions of faith in both an oppositional and celebratory way. Also to reconnect faith with reality, the mythic or symbolic figures of a martyr such as Saint Wojciech with the human figure.

As communist governments are not renowned for their liberal attitudes towards creative expression, there is an expectation that 'unofficial' artists from Eastern Europe will make protest art or political art.

I hate the situation in Poland for this reason. Many things in Poland are lost, because of this way of thinking. For example when you use red it is seen as political. Natural colours have lost their natural meaning. It is crazy, and maybe the reason why I have escaped to neutral colours. In Poland everyone has a very easy way of translating colour - black means death, white means the white eagle on the flag, red is its blood and so on. I do not want to play this artistic game.

I guess every artist faces this, in the West red and white could mean Coca-Cola. Everything is always loaded.

There is a difference. Red means communism. It is a heavier weight then the red of Coca-Cola. Coca-Cola did not murder quite so many people. You must believe in politics to make political art. But I never wanted to be a politician.

Do you think that life in Poland today, where there is virtual economic anarchy, and a reaction against collectivisation, breeds solipsism, promotes a desire to cut off the world and become introspective?

It frightens me to see Polish people take the Western model of life with all the mistakes, the sweet mistakes of the West, the car, the house, the life. They don't want a humanist democracy, they want a Western one. It is a frightening situation.

Artists in the West stand at the edge of a very well defined 20th century tradition of art - perhaps most significantly that of Modernism. In some ways this provides the backdrop or frame of reference to their work. Do you see yourself as being part of or standing against any particular tradition?

My training was very academic, very realist. None of my teachers had any part in postwar or contemporary European art. In a way it's a lonely situation. I have stronger feelings towards ancient art, particularly Egyptian art. But I have no strong connections with any specifically Polish artistic movements, perhaps more to Russian constructivism or to Dadaists like Schwitters.

The sense of theatre, of an austere, poetic stage set is reminiscent of a great figure in performance, that is Kantor. Do you have affinities with him?

I would say that unlike Kantor, my theatre is without actors. It is really more private. Kantor became an artist during the war. The war divided his life into two periods: before and after the war. His base in the childhood was cut off, while mine still exists. Every day I walk in the paths of the past. You could say Kantor's work is informed by the aesthetic of the posed black and white family portrait of the beginning of the century. Mine on the other hand comes out of the ill defined amateur snapshot of the '50s and '60s, essentially grey.

But one of the many dualities in your work is between the economy of gesture, between the individualised privacy of the Venice installation and its evocation of a big emotion, of a collective pathos, of memory and hope. It encapsulates therefore a past and a future.

Contemporary time does not exist, we cannot catch the continuous. As we move ever into the future we are always based in the past. This is the state of my sculpture, there is heat from this pillow, and it's impossible to catch, this continuous flow. As soon as you touch it it's colder than it was at its source. Everything we touch is coming from the past, it's our access to death. For me the important thing in my art is to try to catch that consciousness of life.

Interviewed by Iwona Blazwick, Amsterdam, 12 September 1990

Dry Aqueducts 1990
190 x 45 x 80
190 x 45 x 80
190 x 45 x 80 cm
patinated wood, tinplate

164 x 64 x 94 cm (detail) 1990
wood, concrete, electric pillow

164 x 64 x 94 centimetres (detail) 1990

over:
164 x 64 x 94 cm (detail) 1990
installation Venice Biennale, Aperto 1990

Man with white shirt and black trousers 1990
painted poplar
130 cm high

Stephan Balkenhol

Little Man and Giraffe 1990
painted pine
151 cm high

As we are in London I wanted to ask you about your visit to the British Museum which I believe was very important to you?

The sculptures there that impressed me most were the Egyptian ones. I am fascinated by their aura of eternity and tranquillity. They seem to combine both: they emanate transcendence as well as reality and presence. There is almost something contemporaneous about them. Yet they are not realistic in the way of Roman sculptures which are more like three-dimensional photos.

So you understand realism not in the sense of mimesis or imitation?

I think the key to the question is that sculpture of all periods is always an embodiment of the ideas of the time; making sculpture is a way of appropriating reality. By looking at sculpture you can make deductions about the maker's consciousness of reality.

Did you always want to make figurative sculpture?

It seemed an obvious thing to do. I think if anybody begins to make art, they perhaps start by drawing a figure or sculpting a head.

But the climate of the '70s, when you were studying, was unsympathetic to the human figure in art.

I began by making Pop Art and Assemblages. When I studied in Hamburg I broke with this because there were other influences. It was necessary to deal with the substantial question of what it means to make either figurative or non-figurative work. At that time not much figurative work was being made.

Your teacher in Hamburg was Ulrich Rückriem, whose austere and abstract stone sculptures are obviously very different from your work. Could you describe the influence he had on you?

Perhaps his and my work are like the opposite ends of the same thing. But I don't want to compare myself to Rückriem. The question is whether you want to make a picture of a man in either painting or sculpture, or you don't. But even in Rückriem's work there is a relation to man in the way his sculptures reflect proportions.

But the monolithic structure of your work could also be related to Rückriem, in the way that your figures always emerge from the single block of wood, including their plinth. Also, your sculptures, like Rückriem's, tell the story of how they're made, leaving traces of the process.

I think that comparison goes too far. Rückriem taught me a lot about how to treat materials. It's important to get a feeling for the material.

Why did you choose to use wood? Was it pragmatism or does it have a symbolic connotation for you?

Primarily for pragmatic reasons. You can get hold of it more easily than stone, and wood is particularly well suited to be painted. As a material it is not as important, not as loaded as stone. And finally it has to do with a personal affinity.

The aspect of craftsmanship seems important in your work. All the sculptures are made by yourself and not executed by assistants.

Of course. Every stroke or cut is a decision, and I can't delegate these decisions. But the marks left by the chisel are not intended to show my working process.

An interesting duality in your work is that between the individual, solitary person and society or the crowd. There is a strange frustration connected with it: each time you try and pin down an individual identity, the face merges back into a more collective form of expression.

I believe in the possibility of creating a reality, and I believe it is possible to generate a charged relationship between the spectator and the sculpture. I make figures which are not specific people, they are neither portraits nor self portraits. They could be anybody. It is perhaps even more complex. I think you can make a realistic figure which generates abstract feelings in the spectator.

Is that what you meant when you said on another occasion that you see your sculptures as also possessing an abstract dimension?

Yes, of course. I try to make something other than just sculpted wood.

Traditionally, figurative work has tended to be either populist and kitsch, monumental and political, or expressionistic and shamanistic. Your sculptures are none of this, but seem to occupy a territory all of their own.

The question for me is how is it possible to make figurative work today in the face of the long tradition of realistic sculpture. Sculpture apart from being sculpture has always been used in the past as a vehicle to convey religious or political messages. They always had to transport something other than themselves. At the beginning of the 20th century a movement towards greater autonomy started, which amongst other developments led to the demise of the figurative tradition as a whole. There were only a few good sculptors, like Giacometti or Gonzalez for example, who continued. In the discourses of the '60s and '70s art began to constantly reflect itself, its own means and functions were taken apart and analysed separately: colour and material, form and content etc. I believe that it is important to experience all these parts as a whole.

Are you creating a sculpture about the contemporary human condition?

I don't want to fix the work to just one meaning, or let the sculpture tell a certain story. They are not illustrations of ideas.

One could argue (as Jeff Wall does), that the way art became only about objects was by its nature alienating, because you were no longer able to recognise your body in those objects. The body had been replaced by things.

If I make a sculpture it's like making a proposal to start a conversation. Certainly my sculpture has a particular identity, look or expression, but I want to leave it open. I also like to retain the possibility that the feelings you experience may change when you look at it at different times.

A more specific expression of emotions would perhaps make them more into caricatures. And yet the expression they do have is very important: reduced and boundless at the same time.
Your decisions about size are obviously very important. Why are none of your sculptures life-size?

It's necessary to differentiate between human-size and sculpture-size, to clearly map out an imaginative space. People should never think when they see a sculpture: 'There's a standing man!' Sculpture which is not life-size seems to activate the space in which it is placed more. Also, it engages your imaginative powers much more. Life-size sculptures seem somehow less important.

You have been using two words which I think are really crucial for your work: space and place. How do you see your figures relating to the space in which they stand?

For the Münster Sculpture project (1987) for example I placed a figure against an empty wall of a house. When you make such a marriage between space and sculpture you create a specific location out of a general place. You would not have noticed this place before, but the sculpture activated it.

The little figure you showed in the Tyne International in Newcastle earlier this year seemed remarkable, because in spite of its size it generated an immense sensation of weight and therefore acted very much as an anchor in that room.
Your early figures were nudes. Why did you decide to dress them and how do you choose their clothes?

I originally made nudes because I wanted to understand the human body anatomically. But as you normally don't encounter people in the nude I dress my figures in ordinary, everyday clothes.

Also, most of your figures are standing figures. There's a passage from Elias Canetti's book Crowds and Power, *which is reminiscent of the ideas that surround your work: "Someone who has been standing for a long time expresses a capacity for endurance and resistance. Either because, like a tree he stands firmly in one place or because he allows all of himself to be seen without fear. The stiller he stands, the less often he turns and looks about him, the more impressive he is. If there is a space between the standing man and those around him, the effect he makes is enhanced. Particularly impressive is a man who stands isolated by himself, facing many others but somehow detached from them."*
You seem to have reached a decision consciously to create the effects that are described here about endurance and resistance, about standing apart, but standing with authority.

Of course the position of a figure is part of the expression of the whole. In the standing figures I'm interested in creating an ambiguity between complete stillness and potential movement. But not all my figures stand, this year I made a sitting one, reflecting like Rodin's *Thinker*. The important thing for me is not so much what kind of position they have, as long as the position appears natural and self-evident. I also don't only create solitary figures, I've made compositions of three or more.

What role do the reliefs play in your work?

I enjoy working in a variety of ways, and the relief is a classical sculptural genre. What interests me particularly about the relief is the trompe l'oeil effect: you pretend there is more volume and plasticity than there really is.

Your painted reliefs of heads reminded us very much of recent photography, say the work of Thomas Ruff but also the large portraits of Jeff Wall. Do you feel there is a connection?

Jean-Christophe Amman described the reliefs as 'polaroids in wood'. Sometimes my sculptures capture a momentary impression and that perhaps connects them with photography. Also the square format of some of the portraits might be reminiscent of photography.

I'm not saying your sculpture is photographic, but I do think it's sculpture in the age of photography.

No, I don't see it like that. Perhaps you got that idea when you looked at the reliefs but I am very interested in fundamentally sculptural concerns, in the notion of a volume in a space; so in that respect it's the opposite of photography.

In a recent discussion about your work it was remarked that this was a particularly interesting moment for a German sculptor to make a standing figure, as it is almost the first time since the 1940s that a figure was not either turned upside down or fragmented.

You must consider that I wouldn't have made the work I'm doing now at any other time. Also, I think it was very good for me to have artists as teachers who don't work figuratively such as Rückriem. Because in that situation you ask different and fundamental questions. I recently visited art schools in several German towns. The students worked in a figurative manner, but all had problems with it, because they were taught in traditional academic ways.

It's really fascinating because initially abstraction was related to the human body, and most abstract sculptors will still go back to the human body in some way, and now you are talking about figurative sculpture which needs abstraction or the discipline of minimalism as a base!
Why are all the figures of the same age-group, i.e. your own?

Perhaps in this case I am referring to my own experience. If I made old men or children it would become too narrative, too much an illustration of certain ages, to which I cannot relate.

And yet you make animals?

Yes, but I think that everyone who looks at an animal always recognises certain human characteristics, so the process of identification is not really hampered. I think that animals are odd creatures. You can have a cat and be very fond of it, and yet you might look at it at a certain moment and be struck by its total strangeness and suddenly fear it. I want to capture this ambiguity.

You have created an extraordinary image with your sculpture of Little Man and Giraffe. *It's the only time you combine a man and an animal in such a surreal, dream-like way.*

The giraffe sculpture started from a drawing - that gave me the idea. I made the sculpture very fast, in one night, and it's like a sculptural sketch. You can attach stories to it about affection for animals or fear of loneliness, everyone can make their own. I don't wish to interpret it - you can ask a psychologist! There are obviously different moods reflected in my sculptures, some of them are humorous, like the seal balancing a ball, and others are more severe.

All your animals seem to be confined or controlled by humans.

That's not important. I try to put across the particular features and main characteristics of these animals, but it's very difficult because you have to capture the essential ambiguity as well, otherwise it's mere illustration.

Why do you paint your sculptures?

I'm not a painter, and I don't really know much about colour, but I know that it can completely change an expression. Obviously colour emphasises sculptural qualities. But primarily I use colour in a descriptive way to denote shirt, trousers, hair, eyes etc., and in that function it sometimes also makes the wood disappear.

Do you think your work represents a desire to create something elemental?

In a way yes, I want the sculptures to be as simple as possible.

Do you understand your work as essentially optimistic?

Yes, but in a quiet way.

Interviewed by Iwona Blazwick, James Lingwood and Andrea Schlieker, London, 21 September 1990

Small relief (woman) 1990
painted poplar
24 x 24 x 4 cm

Small relief (man) 1990
painted poplar
24 x 24 x 4 cm

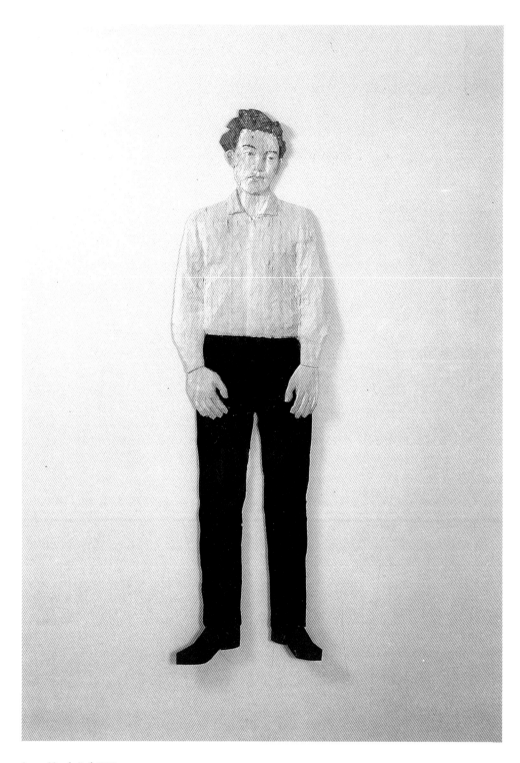

Large Man (relief) 1990
painted poplar
224 x 70 x 4 cm

Cockerel 1990
padouk wood
200 cm high

Jean-Marc Bustamante

When did you start photographing landscapes?

I was assistant to the photographer William Klein, so I spent much of my time printing in the darkroom. I bought a large plate camera with which to carry out some experiments; to leave the darkroom and go outside. The first idea was to find a territory for the photography - not to choose a subject, but to confront myself with a territory. I chose Spain because I was born in Toulouse; my father is Argentinian, perhaps also because of the colour and the quality of the earth. I began to go there every three months with my big camera, around Barcelona or the Costa Brava where the landscapes are not so nice, a landscape where there has been a lot of destruction, a landscape that isn't natural, where nature is no longer wild.

So this was against Klein's preoccupation with incident and event?

I wanted to investigate whether it was possible to make a photograph like a *tableau*. The term in French is precise, because not all paintings are *tableaux*. The closest equivalent in English is the word picture. When I speak of a *tableau*, I am not making a direct reference to painting. The *tableau* is first and foremost an object of thought which resists analysis and has a unique relation to the spectator, the photograph is an object without memory, without narrative. My photographs are not fixed images, they don't fix one subject. The camera is the first architecture, you see the landscape through the camera.

When you talk about these landscapes, you seem to be talking about structural relations that you might find within a picture and not within a particular landscape.

My initial question was - is it possible to produce photographs with the value of *tableaux*? The question was posed at a particular time, in the late 1970s, when there were really two groups of photographers, creative photographers; with all their problems against art and so on, and conceptual artists who used photography as a trace or a measure. With these artists, the status of the *tableau* gives the photograph the greatest possible autonomy.

So you were distancing yourself from a subjective expression?

Yes, I wanted to keep my distance but also to make a good quality image, large format and colour, but without exploiting the colour.

What is the continuing importance of photography in your work now?

It's interesting to analyse this. In 1980 I met Bernard Bazile, a sculptor, and he was very interested in my photographs and I was very interested in his work. We decided to experiment together - it gave me the opportunity to confront images and three-dimensional pieces. This very active collaboration enabled us to explore codes, symbols, images, and to experiment with the image as material. The limitations of the work became apparent quite quickly however; the system could slip into an imagery where irony and cynicism could prevent any real investigation. I wanted to go beyond the image, to exceed it. Looking at my photographic *tableaux* I realised that they contained within them a possible development. In my photographs made over a number of years of indistinct landscapes, transitory or unstable spaces, the outskirts of towns, undefined architectures, I saw several preoccupations. I had frozen a slow movement, that of the earth, but also the process of "decivilisation". All my work at the moment is a continuation of these investigations.

You also use found objects and found photographs.

Found objects very rarely, and then as cultural traces, and found photographs in a specific system of presentation, the *Lumières* which I began in 1989. These are unique black and white seriagraphs on perspex, placed in front of the wall. It's found photography, but it doesn't exist without the wall behind. It produces something like a floating image, the image works through the architecture, the whiteness, the walls, the support; the wall is a setting for the image. It reveals the image.

This raises the question of the relationship between installation and autonomous sculptures or pictures. In the exhibition at Museum Haus Lange in Krefeld, 1990, the relationship between the works, the relationship of the configuration of works to the interior and exterior space was as important as the objects themselves. You have said that you consider your works as autonomous objects. But do they also require a certain anonymity so that these relations between each other, and with the space, can be created?

I like that relationship with the thing that's there - maybe it's art, maybe it's not. I was interested in creating such feelings in Haus Lange. They weren't overwhelming pieces. I'd like to produce a work which you can walk past without immediately noticing. I couldn't consider Mies van der Rohe's house as a neutral space. Having stayed there for some time, the architecture became a very strong presence, and I decided to make this new work. In organising the space, I gave to each piece a discrete yet unavoidable presence. They retained their autonomy, they did not emphasise their difference to the place. The relationship of the *tableau* to its model is similar.

Would they need to have some quality of the ordinary?

Yes, but it is also important to assert the presence of the object. It's closed, self-contained. It can desire the viewer, or it can exist on its own.

Many of your sculptures feel condensed or closed in on themselves. But how far can you push this without then reformulating the reductive closure of Minimalism?

In my opinion, there is always a kind of desire to step back, to be at a distance, in my art but also in my life. The reference to minimalism remains possible. I wanted to make reference to those who have established a vocabulary in the 20th century, a vocabulary which has enabled me to develop another kind of complexity, from Vuillard and Matisse to Minimalism.
The choice of material is very important to me. It's not sophisticated material, it's very rough, it's oak, not an exotic wood... it's important for me to come back to primary materials. For me the confrontation with death is very important. My reference is more Carl Andre than Donald Judd.

André is concerned with questions of death as well?

Death , and also the physical approach of the viewer. You can't get inside my works. I think it's very important to examine the relationship between the viewer and the piece, and at the same time to create a distance between the object, and the eye of the viewer. I would like to try and create an immediate emotional relationship between the viewer and the piece, the recognition of a familiar image.

You just made an enormous leap. You started talking about material and its specificity, and somehow that transformed into a statement about death. Could you explain that relationship?

I think the viewer knows primary materials. Wood is domestic, so is sand, earth - so there's an emotional response and I'd like to keep that immediacy of recognition. I don't want to make different images, new forms, but to start out from primary and organised things... for me the problem of vision is more important, perhaps because of my training as a photographer.

Is there a sense of trying to recuperate things which can't be recuperated?

I think there is a degree of melancholy. I'm very interested in images of schools, and I'm making some new *Lumières* of schools, platforms,

corridors, staircases, playgrounds. But it's not nostalgia. These are some of the first things you know, the things that stay with you... the space of the playground, the struggle for life in the playground.

Why do you say that you don't want to create something new?

It's not intended to be provocative, just a reaction against superficial radicality. I met Donald Judd in Bern, and we talked about innovation and artwork at the end of the century. It was very difficult talking to Judd about this problem because he said you have to do something new, you have to innovate, you must have a radical attitude etc. It's a different question for my generation. The desire for radicality is no longer a way of creating specific worlds, new visions of things. For artists, "innovation" should be the standpoint for a new relationship to the world and not simply to art. I think that as the world mutates, art should change. We are all part of the same history. The rules change, we are today within a new order. The individual should understand before anything else that he should have a close, intimate relationship with others. We don't go forward anymore, we work with what is there. Art is no longer in a state of progress, but one of induction.

You can reorganise things, reproduce them, change them about...

Maybe that attitude is radical now. We're living in a very interesting time. The '60s in France were preoccupied with theories. Now it's more open, richer, more human, there are more possibilities. Nowadays there is a space for sensibility, pure emotion, it is less cerebral. But in France they are more disposed to cerebral things, they want a precise system. I can't say I have a system or a theory.

Does that make your position more difficult in France?

I get much more of a response to my work abroad than in France. In France, there is a fascination with intelligence. Intelligence put to the service of art can produce some very intense works, but for the most part it leads to very rarefied things. Look at Duchamp. Everyone likes him for his ready mades, his word-plays, his brilliance at chess, but they forget the rest... Look at Buren, who is liked for his rigour, his decors. I like Buren when I think of Cadère. But the disciples of Duchamp and Buren are like sad orphans. They make art as if it was something technological, like scientific experiments. It's a great shame that it has got so specialised.

Can you say something about the positioning of your work in the space. You talked a litttle about it when we walked through your exhibition at ARC in Paris and you suggested that you organised different configurations to prompt different readings. Do you have a system which is deliberately heterogeneous, even anti-systematic?

It is important for me to plan my work so that it is not necessarily immediately visible. Sometimes I deliberately place art behind the viewer. I don't like works of art to provide order. The relationship between the viewer and the work is important - each time a different relationship, a new order. So it's important for me to construct the arrangement of the pieces beforehand, their inter-relations. It's interesting to mix different kinds of work for example in Krefeld the *Bac à Sable*, two landscapes, *Lumières*... to see how far you can go without telling a story. I'm always afraid because the creation of the piece must visually resist any kind of narrative in its materials and its forms.

So you don't privilege one particular reading?

Perhaps I do, but without being aware of it. I like to work with simple, basic things that everyone knows more or less.

The associations of domesticity were very strong in Krefeld and this encouraged some narration through the rooms in the sense of an abstracted personal history. The photograph of the school classroom, almost deserted, with a strong minimal grid of desks broken only by the presence of one or two boys, this seemed like an introduction to reading the group of works you had placed.

I haven't any lessons to teach, any answers, any philosophy. I want to make objects with autonomy. It's important for people to be able to read the work on many levels. I try to make a work that's fairly simple and very complicated. I try to layer things so that all kinds of readings are possible, but none amongst them could be isolated. You have to find a perfect weight, a balance between three considerations - the phenomenological, which is to say the establishment of a system of reconstitutions, the iconological, and the ontological or the question of otherness. None of these three should be dominant. This creates a sedimentation where the work lives and measures itself with the real. There is an osmosis here, and the work either asserts itself or disappears.

You said that in your landscapes you were trying to find a place that is in some ways a non-place. Does that continue into your sculptures, like Vercruysse's Atopies, for example?

I see Vercruysse as being at the same time more detached from the real and yet rooted in his origins. I feel more involved in transitory places and uncertain origins. In a text on my photographs, Alain Cueff

opposed the walk in the landscape of British artists to the sense of displacement in my work. "Not to have been there, not to have stayed there, but to have fallen from the sky, snatched something and disappeared." The titles of my recent works are significant here, *Aller Retour, Ici Là*, or more earthy ones like *Bac à Sable* or *Sac à Dos*.

When you talk about the specificity of materials and the heterogeneity of your work, are you trying to escape a fixed image of yourself as a creator ?

No, the works are charged and tensed, with the greatest possible emphasis on the viewer. Perhaps you can recognise a Bustamante in this sense, through its tonality, its state of mind, through the relationship with the world, with reality more than with something formal.

Interviewed by James Lingwood and Andrea Schlieker, London, 4 July 1990

page 34
Paysage 1990

Bac à sable 1990
installation ARC, Paris

over:
Lumières 1990
installation ARC, Paris, 1990

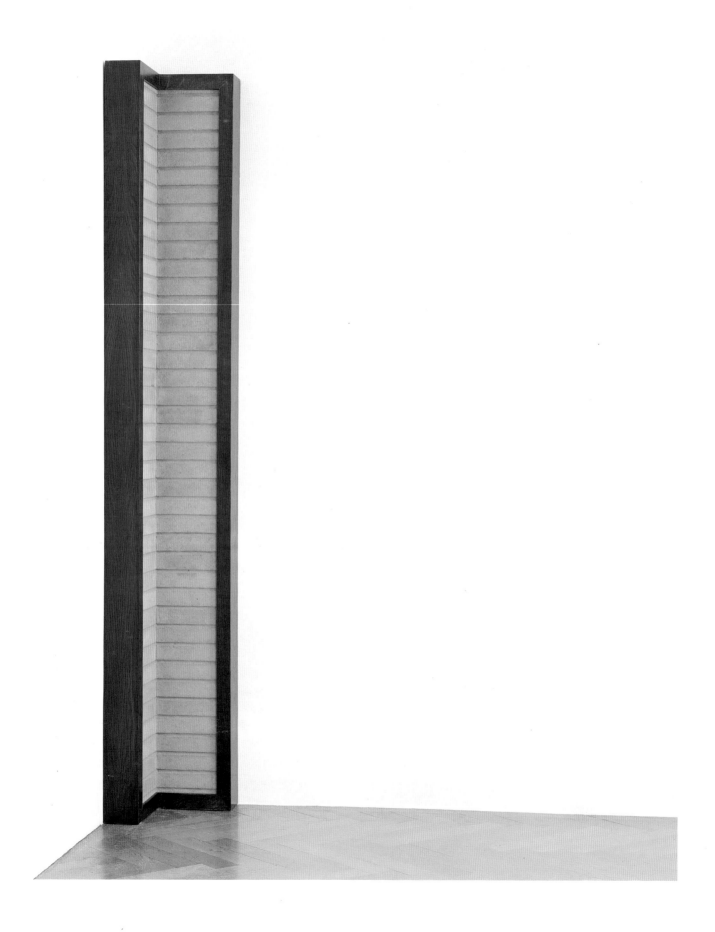

Interieur I and *Paysage Minium II* 1988
installation Kunsthalle Bern, 1989

left:
Paysage 1990
installation Museum Haus Lange, Krefeld

Untitled 1990

right:
Inventaire 1989
installation de Appel, Amsterdam 1990

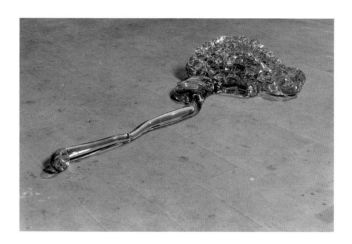

Untitled 1990
solid glass 36 x 96 x 289 cm

Asta Gröting

Materiality is a central aspect of your work - you repeatedly play with the contrasts between organic and synthetic, artificial and natural, crude and sophisticated.

It isn't a method. I choose the most suitable material for the expression of an idea. Glass in the case of the digestive system at Venice, for example, or rubber - any kind of material. In the acrylic wall-pieces I've used a brazil nut, or sunflower seeds, preserved for eternity, but rendered useless by the embalming process. But the genetic information will exist for ever.

This touches upon another dialectic in your work: with the nut you are introducing the idea of the microcosm while at the same time you are referring to the macrocosm of an industrial system.

I often use the interplay of large and small. That's what sculpture consists of, the relationship between large and small.

The brazil nut is an unusual choice of object. The way it is floating within the acrylic is reminiscent of something like a reliquary, lending it a sacred, transcendental aura.

I chose the brazil nut because it is the biggest and most sculptural seed I could find. I wanted to show the way an object would appear if it was reduced in scale. I see the nut both as an abstract sculptural form and as the embodiment of the notion of 'seed'.

But when you say 'seed' are you basically thinking in terms of growth?

That isn't the only thing. There's the genetic information and the idea of growth - the brazil nut would grow if you planted it. The piece of concrete behind the nut was found in the street and mirrors the nut's form. The nut itself is very precise, the enlargement very imprecise. One reason for choosing the nut is simply that it was a suitable form to create the impression as if the concrete had been reduced in size, compressed and condensed. And embedded in this compression lies the seed that could expand and grow.

Is that a kind of comment about precision in nature, imprecision in culture?

No. I would rather my work didn't provide comments upon things, or if it does then it's in the mind of the individual viewer. But perhaps it can be seen as a comment upon the impossibility of producing precise images or of representing accumulated information, also the impossibility of representing nature.

But there is a desire to make the forms as beautiful and precise as possible. Beauty seems to be an important aspect of your work.

The material is there to visualise my personal ideas and feelings. I never choose my material for its beauty. For me the state of beauty consists of tension and a wealth of associations.

Is the way you use materials a reflection on the tradition of Arte Povera, or does it mirror personal experience?

Debates about the problematic of the previous artistic generation impressed me very much when I started to make art. But it is not enough to say that I deal with Arte Povera issues because I use those types of materials. My criteria for selection are other than to look for elementary or even poetic materials. Also, it has nothing to do with form-analysis. It has to do with that which is visible but cannot be explained, or at least not in terms of Arte Povera - for I'm equally concerned with the work of Michelangelo or Rodin. Also, my technical training at Hoesch, a large steel producing and processing plant, taught me a way of handling material, a certain generosity. But of course also the industrial area where I grew up, the Ruhrgebiet, acted as a general influence.

Not only the materials but also some of the shapes you are using, especially in your older work - appear to have overt sexual connotations.

Sexuality is not the subject matter that I want to explore in my work. I don't want to visualise sexuality. There are organic and biological and physical aspects to the work, it can be erotic. But it is an eroticism that is generated by the material, erotic in the sense of 'concerning the senses'.

Why are you producing these digestive systems?

From the earlier conveyor-belt works I developed the desire to make a 'human conveyor-belt'. That is why I combined (in Venice) the large wheels of a yellow conveyor-belt - a material used in mining to transport coal - with the human stomach made of glass. I use glass because it symbolises a fluid, liquid material. A digestive system, too, is constantly moving - it processes and produces, similar to human activity in general.

I'd like to look at the transition from this kind of non-figurative sculpture to works showing organic parts of the body. A lot of work in the '60s, such as that of Nauman or Serra, was discussed in terms of the body, in phenomenological terms.

Nauman's work now includes very direct images of the body, while I work in a more distanced and abstract way.

But was the transition to working on the human body difficult for you?

I don't work with the human body as such. I am interested in relating to an organic process. The idea originated from the identification of a digestive system with a human conveyor-belt. If I hadn't made that connection I would never have been interested in representing elements of the human body.

In historical terms the idea of endless forms, like Brancusi's Endless Column, *has a spiritual dimension. Now here - both in the conveyor-belt and digestive system pieces - you are making work with the idea of an endless process, but eliminating any spiritual reference in order to concentrate on material.*

I don't think about the spiritual, but rather about the industrial. Most of my sculptures represent or express concrete physical and psychological states that represent all of human activity, feelings etc.

Activity ends when the factory closes down or the human being dies. There's a sense in which a feeling of death or embalming pervades the work.

I'm interested in what death is, because for instance usually you only see a digestive system when you see a dead person opened up. You'll never see your own.

Also, you have represented a stopped 'industrial process' with the digestive system, as well as with the large wheels - it now circles endlessly around itself, while the original conveyor-belt is horizontal.

Here I made the sculpture based on the inherent meaning of the material.

How important is the placement of the individual works in relation to each other within a given space, of establishing a specific reading, a definite system of reference?

That is always important. But they also act as autonomous objects. When I make an exhibition I try and bring some life into it, add a narrative dimension. The different systems I work with tell different stories. For example, it matters which direction the conveyor-belt faces in relation to the digestive system. There is always a tension in my installations. I make the wall-mounted works and the floor-based works in tandem.

Many of your answers suggest you want to create an open work.

I don't want to make excuses for my work by saying that it expresses something specific. It simply exists. It isn't a visualisation of social systems, it's about being in space.

Do your sculptures consciously refer to the value of labour, alluding specifically to the industrial worker, the glass-blower etc?

Not expressly, but for example the small, handmade stitches on the large wheels are very meditative, and that's important. I deliberately didn't glue this piece, I sewed it.

Do you want to refer to a particularly female activity with your handsewn stitches?

No - the tailor is a classically male profession, saddles are sewn as well, and shoes. Heavy materials are usually sewn by men.

But you clearly demonstrate a respect for craft in general terms?

Yes. I carve and model parts of my sculptures because it is only within this process of craftsmanship that a form is created which expresses my attitude or emotion in the most precise way. Ideally I'd do it all myself. Things look completely different when they are handmade.

So do you see your work embodying a kind of rescue of craft for our own industrial age?

It isn't about the age so much as my idea of materials - I like to work that way. I don't think it's good for artists simply to farm work out to craftsmen, to commission the whole process. It's a kind of art production I find fundamentally unsympathetic. Ideas get lost along the way. A handmade piece is more intimate, precise, more caring - it's visible in the end result. I rate that higher.

But surely your glass pieces are produced by craftsmen?

But I made a model. I didn't just give them a photograph of an abdominal cavity and tell them to get on with it.

You say you'd like to make everything yourself because it has a higher value - isn't that a curious idea of society? Isn't it rather antisocial?

No, I don't believe that the value of a work of art can be measured by the amount of labour invested. However, autonomy is independence. When I work with companies, they're interested in making money fast.

They often don't care about the quality of the work. Maybe sometimes you can find a craftsman who does that. I like to do it myself because it gives me more control over the end result.

There seem to be echoes here of the ethos celebrated by William Morris and the Arts and Crafts Movement, who in the 19th century were concerned with the craftsman's identification with his own work and with bridging the gap between the so-called lower and higher arts.

Perfectly crafted art is not the main focus of my work, I'm more concerned to create something personal and intimate. Imperfection can be more perfect - the stitches for example aren't perfect. It is to do with energy. When I'm involved in crafting a piece, I materialise my own energy, which I can then experience myself, and that is an identification which others can experience as well. It all expresses a feeling of life, which is what I'd like to convey.

There is a certain non-finito character about your work.

Yes, I find that there is often something inhuman or dead about completeness, about finished industrial products.

If you think about the sculpture of the '80s, much of which was extremely cool and polished...

That was due to a belief in economic growth at that time. I prefer a human system; but there are political interpretations that I would reject. Humanism is already a form of politics. I'd rather leave some things unexplained, you can see it yourself. When you work with clay, when you can see the traces of the artist's fingers, then there's a feeling of life - unlike in polished industrial production. It represents a different sense of life. I am not interested in the repetition of existing patterns.

Do you want to bring humanity back to art?

It's my way into art.

Interviewed by James Lingwood and Andrea Schlieker, Düsseldorf, 4 August 1990

Untitled 1990
silicon, wood-shavings 5.90 x 1.90 m

Untitled 1990
acrylic, brazil nut, concrete, iron

Installation , Venice Biennale, Aperto 1990
solid glass; yellow underground conveyor belt

Three Ballerinas 1990

Juan Muñoz

There are a number of recurring motifs in your work such as floors, balconies and figures - where do they originate from?

The floor developed out of a desire to build something that was real, something people could walk across. I wanted to make a real object, not an object that stands in for reality. It was also a necessary device for locating the figure, that figure that was sitting on a shelf at that time; the floor becomes like a gigantic prop for such a piece. Yet my figures are at the same time indifferent to the floor, and indifferent to the spectator who is in a sense a performer...

So the floor creates a participatory space...?

Well no, it was a device within which to place a figure. At first, works such as the empty balconies were dealing with the absence of the human figure. A very early work I made was a small staircase and a balcony top. As you walk straight onto it you look out. But I wanted to make a work that stands between two positions - between doing nothing and watching, and passing by and being watched.

Another early piece, which has an open flick knife attached to the back of the bannister, also introduces a sense of violence. The unease is all the more profound, as hand rails are usually a sign of security or comfort, something to lean on.

Very few people saw the flick knife. I was very interested in this idea of the work, inviting your hand to go out, and then the idea of danger, of uncertainty. Do you really need a handrail to go up the stairs, or is it just a reassuring image? These bannisters are very strongly related to the body and to the passageway, to going through. They come from that moment when you lean on a balcony; I wanted to flatten the handrails so that they become useless, and at the same time pressed up against the wall like that, they look like a balcony, they even share the same wooden structure at the top.

The bannister, attached to the gallery wall, articulates a language which is close to that of minimalism. But the switch blade, cuts through that language quite violently. Does this signify a general desire to cut through the formalist language?

There is just a fear of a tendency to become formalist. It is dangerous to make a piece, and then to try and make endless variations of it. In order to make it interesting, you have to put yourself in a position to say it is the last one, and to destroy.

Your work is characterised by a configuration of elements rather than the discrete object. There is a unity that is achieved through

the 'autonomous object' of a classical tradition of sculpture, or the unity of fragments suggested by artists such as Beuys or Kounellis, a tradition which you side with. But now you are discarding certain elements in your work such as the floor, and are going back to making a statue. Does that mean you are trying to create another sort of unity based on a single object?

I don't seem to be able to make a statue without a base, its plinth. Looking at monuments in the street the sculpture is made of bronze, the plinth is made of granite and they end up looking like the whole thing is made of one material. I am not suspicious of the single art object leaning against a white wall, but I could not make the figure without the floor, I could not see the general without the plinth and the cars passing by. It's not so much that fragments are being put together, it is more the impossibility of finding anything that has not been fragmented already. I think that the glue of history is so powerful that if you want to separate two parts you will always break something. You can never separate the glueing moment of history, you cannot separate the bronze general from the plinth, from the asphalt, from the cars that pass it by, from the hundred year old trees next to it, from the boredom it represents and from the anonymity which is the consequence of the passage of time.

Using the specific example of that context, how do you relate the drawings to the sculptures?

To draw is a pleasure, it is a very beautiful, solitary job. I always draw. I never wanted to draw the pieces I was making because I thought they would be like illustrations. So I always try to make drawings that are separate entities. I have made drawings of rooms, of backs and other parts of the body. With the black drawings I wanted to draw the back and make it very beautiful, enticing yet giving nothing away.

But do you see them as a necessary extension of the three dimensional works?

I do not find it necessary that sculpture should be a free standing object. I think it is all part of a larger discourse. If you look at more of the drawings, they cannot really be separated from the rest of the work.

Going back to the origin of the motifs in your work, it seems very rooted in Spanish vernacular traditions.

Well, I hate the idea of someone saying, ah this is a Spanish balcony, I do not think that is the original source of the work. Of course it is undeniable that Beuys was German, that Goya was Spanish. But this is like an awareness of your own condition. For me the balcony is a reality not an invention. And certainly for a Swede to make a balcony would be an extremely foreign image, like me making an iceberg.

But what is interesting is that your work transcends the specificity of place or cultural identity or history. Apart from evoking a particular Spanish Baroque, it also represents a typology of form and can therefore trigger a collective response. When you wrote about the Baroque spaces of Borromini you describe them as 'Where God is just about to appear, whence He has just departed, or from where His appearance has been absurdly delayed'. There is the same sense of absence in your work.

I sometimes feel that my recent work is about waiting, waiting for something to happen that might never happen; on the other hand afraid in case it does happen, or even wishing it had never occurred. It is like keeping a work at that state we would call desire - keeping it at that level of desire, just holding it there, that wish, that uncertainty, keeping the work still just there. Or like watching a door which one day a person might open.

There's a kind of paradox here, when you introduced the figure with the floor it only served to accentuate rather than retrieve the sense of loss. The figure tends to create a more desolate social space than the empty balcony.

Well, I cannot make a figure that is personalised. I don't seem to be able to make a person that I know. Because of this 'otherness' of figures like the dwarf I think they create a wide distance between the spectator and the object. They disappear away. About loss I can say with the utmost arrogance, I have no nostalgia whatsoever about anything. I don't think anything was ever lost. If I deal with the passage of time, it's because I have to grow from history. My work deals with history, with an awareness of my condition today and the fragments of memory.

But if these are images and spaces that deal with marginalised figures, like the dwarf, or people who are performing for culture, like a ballerina, what are they saying about the state of contemporary culture if it is not about a certain loss or an absence?

I feel that when I was making the ballerina it was more about endlessly moving, but always finding herself in the same space. I thought that when I made the ballerina it was a courageous act, to put forward such a permutated, even weak image, such a secondary presence.

The ballerinas have no legs, they rock on round bases, standing and not standing...

They are about going nowhere. I was very concerned with the floor, about its relation to the base, about what happens above and below and this seemed a perfect solution. The work is both the solution and the search for it, the pacing about, the working out of a problem. The ballerina is about the possibility of moving about and of hope, of conviction and lack of conviction, impossibility, uncertainty... This work is about a presence, but I don't think it is commenting on the social environment. I want to make a statue, not a sculpture.

Why is it that your figures are always approximations of the human body, but never the human itself, there are toys, shadow figures, ventriloquist dummies... You began by introducing limbs but they were the limbs of a puppet or a marionette.

It is not to do with toys, but more to do with 'otherness'. I talked to many friends in Madrid to see if they knew where I could find a dwarf. Someone advised me to go to this bar, and talk with a waiter who knew a man called George. I went and left my number and he called me. We arranged to meet. He asked me how he would recognise me, and I thought, that's the right question, he is putting me in the position that I am putting him in. In a way I was terrified by this question. When I cast his face, it was covered in a white blanket, and plaster - it made a horrific image. But it would never be him. I would not demean George, or myself. I do not reproduce any real human beings. When I made the hunter figures, I wasn't representing a specific person, I was trying to make an image of a man walking nowhere.

It cannot be a coincidence that you are choosing figures, such as the ventriloquist's dummy or the Prompter *that are mute, or have no voice of their own. Is that a metaphorical statement about the human condition?*

Yes, it's true that those works are related to sound and language, or the absence of language. But when I made the *Prompter* I wanted to make a house of memory, the mind you never see but is always there. It is a little like the theatre of Giulio Romano or Bruno, like a stage set with no representation, no play, only one man trying to remember, trying not to forget. More a relation with history. There are different ways of approaching the figure which I am trying to make coherent. My work is made very slowly and tranquilly. It is made coldly, dispassionately yet ends up feeling painful. These monuments of generals have no story, no particular meaning, nobody remembers what they did. They stand there and become perfectly invisible in the city.

Are you saying that the precondition of a monument in the 20th century is that it is anonymous and can be invested with almost any meaning?

Recently walking through Paris I saw again the monument to Balzac. It is placed in a square where thousands of people pass by and never look at it because they might think it is just another sculpture. Looking at this sculpture by Rodin one may regard it as a work by a significant French sculptor, one may regard it as important because of the writer it depicts; at the same time it merges with its background, as if it had always been there; I like this sense of indifference towards our time. I am not talking about progress or investing an already overloaded work with more meaning, I am talking or walking in the city and looking.

In the way that your works are never recognisable human figures, - 'stand-ins' like puppets or ballerinas, even backs - do they function as ciphers in the way that you say monuments in the 20th century are empty, so that you can fill them with meaning according to which of the many citizens you are? That you want neutrality so that the spectator can conjecture what is in the front of that back, or what identity the puppet is acting out?

I'm not really concerned with the spectator when I make the work, but I do try to leave a big gap; I try to leave a degree of error, a sort of crack at the bottom of the door, where you might be able to sneak through if you're interested in getting something from the work. The ballerina interested me in this depiction of standing/not standing. At the same time someone might just get an image of beauty from it. I put a lot of care and attention into making the back of the ballerina. I tried to be as sensual as possible in a space of 25 centimetres. I don't want to close off the piece.

So what informs your desire to make figures? Is it something to do with trying to reconstruct subjectivity or is it more specific?

I want to be able to make a man, a man in a room. I want to make an autonomous statue but I don't seem to be able to.

Do you consider them grotesque?

Sometimes there is a need to create some inner violence in the work. When I made the first ballerina, I wanted to put a switch blade in one of her hands.

And what determines the scale of both the figures and the objects? We have talked about monuments but all the figures are small, less than human size.

I don't think you can make things the size that you are, they have to be bigger or smaller. I make them smaller because I feel that creates a wider physical and conceptual distance between the spectator and the object.

I know you resist definition through national traits but these small 'grotesques', particularly the dwarf, also have their place in a specifically Spanish tradition, from Velasquez to Buñuel.

The dwarf is a constant image of the Baroque period. You find it in a lot of Italian painting, even Japanese movies. The dwarf was the only person that could criticise the court. Because of his physical distortion, he was allowed to distort or exaggerate reality. One of the dwarves painted by Velasquez was bought because he had a disease that made him laugh constantly. So they would take him out after dinner and his laughter was so contagious that everyone would laugh, and then they'd get bored and send him home. I'm not exactly denying that there's a Spanish link but it's not conscious. The dwarf was born in my work from a walk in a garden in Munich. Rüdiger Schöttle wanted me to make something around an architectural ruin for his Bestiarium project. So I went to this very Baroque park in Munich and picked up a leaflet about the Rococco architect who designed it and discovered that he had been very small in size, practically a dwarf. And then I knew what I was going to make: the image of a dwarf inside the Prompter box, the *Prompter* is, in a way, the House of Memory and therefore the ruin Rüdiger asked me to do.

What did you mean when you said you wanted to 'pare down the human figure to the degree zero'?

There has got to be a possibility of creating a wider language. When you look at early Renaissance work, when you look at Giotto, you can see the same face repeated almost identically. The Virgin Mary is always the Virgin Mary, not a specific mother, Christ is always Christ, an abstraction. They get de-personalised so they become surreal in a way. A lot of artists have been very lucky - they have had this cipher for a million years, it's been very successful. I think that if I could make a figure that is a nonentity in the same way, I could work for a million years. It is not that I want to make an icon, more the ultimate image. I like to have a problem I can go back to day after day, I like to have this gigantic problem. To have a full store cupboard of possibilities - to have houses, woods, streets, squares, rivers, people and through these sources you can tell everything you feel.

So does the language of Minimalism represent a sculptural language of closure for you?

It's true it was never interesting for me. I came to realise that I could have been walking in a park, or drinking in a bar instead of looking at thousand upon thousand of little boxes. There was not that much to gain from it. I always felt closer to Merz, Anselmo or Kounellis than to Judd, Andre, Morris, Barry or LeWitt. I think what a lot of people today need is an involvement with the real world. Someone like Judd defined a unity, a common element in art. But Borromini created a different 'conceptual unity' to which I am more aligned than the reductivism of the Minimalist project.

Is your work a response to the crisis of confidence in the language of Minimalism in particular or Modernism in general?

It's a mistake to view Modernism as a block without fissures, or cracks.

But the ballerina does seem like a metaphor for the end of a certain period, and the opening up of another one: Of the transition from the nihilistic atmosphere of much art of the 1980s where it seemed that it was impossible to make images any more and where there was only a world of hyper-reality, to a more open future. The ballerina seems to represent both stasis and movement, even action.

Well, I'm always suspicious of dates, I think there were activities which did put forward possibilities, of work where there was denial but also affirmation. In a way to make these definitions of times or movements is like the very thinking process of the Modernist 'central section' which makes these broad generalities. At the same time it is true that a lot of people came into the art world to say there is nothing to be said. And when I first saw in writing that I had described myself as being a storyteller, might have crossed some bridge.

But there are these orthodoxies or preoccupations which dominate certain times. If you talked about being a storyteller ten years ago it would have been very acceptable in a different way from the way it is read today, it would have been interpreted as the reintroduction of narrative into painting. But you seem to be saying something different. You seem to be opening up a different space where you reintroduce aspects of reality or lived experience into the work, into these fissures of the orthodoxy of modernism.

It is true that there is a change in sensibility but it's more to do with being bored with denial. We have become aware of the millions of stories that we did not allow ourselves to tell over the last ten years because of our suspicion of the conditions of expression. Now we know we can express without being expressionistic. The doors are swinging open for everything to occur but I don't know how much of the landscape beyond we are actually going to travel. This whole conversation is about the door being opened, but we are not talking about the distant horizon or even the foreground, we are still talking about the door. And I'm interested in that territory between enclosure and openness. This is the room from which we look out, the room of history and we stand in that space between - call it the landscape of desire, the threshold, the hinges of the door. I can never make art outside of our history. This I know is an impossibility.

What do you expect to find on the other side of the door?

Nothing because my work lacks belief in a way.

One can trace in your work references to a number of traditions or genres in art, such as the still life; and to literary history. Your titles even quote certain writers.

There are authors I have read whose work seems to occur in a silent space somehow. You read Eliot and you have the impression it's a voice in an empty room. I get a similar feeling looking at a work like Seurat's *Bathers* in the National Gallery. The space between all these people looking at the river, there is such a distance between them all. Each one is standing so still. And so mute. And each one seems to be occupying a space of silence. They are placed with perfect equilibrium between them. Looking at it I realised I wasn't interested in the mathematical formulation behind the work. I was interested in the incredible loneliness of the characters. On the other hand no pain, no suffering is described, just the condition of each of them. But it is also a relaxed Sunday scene. I thought: this is the image of the soul looking at the desert. I realise I go back again and again to looking at certain images. In the Seurat there is a position of stillness and muteness combined with an incredible transparency. The indifference of the sunny afternoon is paralleled with a tremendous tension. It's going to take me many years to achieve that quality.

Interviewed by Iwona Blazwick, James Lingwood and Andrea Schlieker, London, 10 July 1990

Dwarf standing on a chair 1990

preceding page:
Sentries 1990

Minaret for Otto Kurtz 1985

Lines of my Hand 1990

Greek Ballerina No II 1989

Black Lemons 1989

Thomas Schütte

Your installation at ARC takes the spectator through a journey;
rather than looking at discrete works on a plinth they experience a
number of different situations.

The installation of work is as important as its production. It's a
separate work in itself. After I have made the work I have nothing else
to do, but to influence how people move, how people look, to find
new combinations of the work.

So the reading of different groups of work changes according to
the way they are juxtaposed in the space?

Even old works take on different formal aspects. It's a complex process
to make installations in rooms - you can't see what's going to work in
advance of actually making the installation. I enjoy dealing with works
as plain materials, it's not unlike decorating a room, even hanging
drawings can be interesting. Drawn lines also define space.

There's an early work where you actually hang garlands around a
room (Rote Girlande, *1979) and another where you use the walls*
to create a pattern of coloured circles (Ringe, *1977/89) This sense*
of decoration seems to continue informing your work.

I separate production from the promotion of decoration - I don't see
decoration in a negative sense. It's one of the most fantastic fields to
work in. What I was attempting to do 13 years ago was to work
without a mechanical system, without grids, or rectangles; to create a
free form, discrete decoration. I was very interested at that time in
non-gallery spaces. I was making lots of things in living and working
places, offices, living-rooms - you have to be able to live with work in
those spaces. It was a typically '70s idea. The work is not crying out to
the public, the public almost didn't see the work. It was a game
between 2 or 3 people. It was not a public decoration.

Were you influenced by the minimalist and conceptual artists
working in the '70s?

Absolutely, yes. People describe the '70s as dry and grey and boring,
dominated by the square. But I see it as the other way round, the '80s
was the most deserted time. It was just so much consumption, so
much production. I'm happy that these stupid years are over. The
artists of the '70s occupy a position today I don't share, but I respect
them a lot. It was this generation that established the grammar, the
training and the language. They address the fundamental problems -
of lighting, material, meaning, and space. Their work is not about
squares. They have developed incredible solutions for these problems
which are impressive in their simplicity and formal conviction.

Yes, your work displays an enormous pluralism of form, material
and technique. Can you say whether there is a single line of
enquiry that unites all your activities?

I like to do many things simultaneously mostly to avoid getting bored.
Also to avoid having to solve certain problems - like getting stuck with
how to make the nose of a horse. I'm not interested in this. The real
problem is knowing why you should continue, of trying to find
something more interesting. The whole show business thing can be a
little bit boring, I mean the repetition and recognition film. The
decorations I made represented a period of research - using simple,
cheap materials, finding easy solutions. And I keep moving from one
form across to another; what I show may not be what I'm working on.
My show at the Kunsthalle Bern was called *Seven Fields*. The title is
really important. I saw the installation as being like a farmer and his
different produce, potatoes, cows, pigs, tomatoes, summer fruits,
chickens... It was a way of laying out all my work, and looking for the
roots of it. I'm partly concerned with the fascination of producing a
work, to bring something into existence. But I don't see my work as
pluralist in the postmodernist sense.. It's just that I'm against this
mono-culture. I try to see one thing from five different view points.
And you keep moving and working around a central point, but what it
is we don't know. Because as soon as you can define it, it's ended.

Is there an autobiographical element in works such as the
architectural models - are they a metaphor for the artist's studio
or do they make a broader statement?

I used a model because this is something everyone understands, it was
an easy way to make a standard sculpture. It's very accessible to a
variety of readings. You can imagine it as the prototype for something
bigger, or as something seen from the child's point of view; you can
see it as a public theatre, and so on. If the work is successful it can
contain everything and can't be split up into single meanings.

The Casino *you are exhibiting in London seems more fantastical*
than your earlier models. It's like something out of a fairy tale. It
doesn't look like a Casino though.

It's called *Casino* because it shares similar design features with the
building on the 50DM banknote; but it isn't a literal representation.
It's a game, played with forms and colour. The drawings underneath
which were made a few years ago, looked to me like casino chips on
baize. Their surface is covered with rings and squares and they would
have looked stupid hung on a wall - there was no right way up or
down. The only solution was to throw them under the table. The
whole piece was made for the shop window of the Fischer gallery so
people could see it from the street.

You have made a number of public works, such as the Ice Cream Pavilion *in Kassel for Documenta, the* Cherry Column *in Münster, or the* Schutzraum (Refuge Space) *in Sonsbeek.*

The last one was a big decoration for a power plant in Germany. I've done a lot of commissions, but I've lost interest. Nobody cares. The people who order these works don't care about the artist or the work; for them it is a kind of city advertisement. The sculpture simply becomes a logo. There's not only a fascination about working with an artist for these city or company people - artists are also cheap. If you ask Saatchi for a campaign you pay the price, but you can buy the artist for a cup of coffee and the cost of production. It's also pointless to disturb people on the street, to make an intervention into a shopping mall, or to compete with commercial decorations.

The streets are already huge exhibition spaces, full of spectacle. The public monument must not only compete, however, it has to be of something. What do you think the monument can embody today?

For me it is not a problem, it's more a question of approach. I don't want to make statements against commerce, against Coca-Cola. The irony is already there in the city, because you are anonymous, nobody cares about you. The idea of city furniture is interesting but it cannot succeed. I think it's very over-rated. Public art simply becomes another standard commodity. The cherries I made on a column - I could just transplant it and mass produce it five times for five different cities. Yet it was made for a specific place. And the situation this piece was specially made for also changed afterwards. I placed a kitsch sculpture in the middle of a car park. But it's not a car park anymore. Now there's an interesting sculpture in the middle of a kitsch place.

The fact that you make models and plans suggests that your work is prescriptive.

My father is an engineer. Engineering plans and models - these are ways of imagining situations. To build. I paint but I am not a painter - if there's no green I'll use blue.

From small models to actual buildings, from tiny figures to huge melons, from little houses to gigantic flags, your work shifts scale all the time. The spectator must constantly re-orientate him or herself, to become like Gulliver travelling from Lilliput to Brobdignag.

I'm a big fan of Swift but I don't see the work as constantly changing. There are just three scales 1:1, 1:5 and 1:20. It's when you put these things together in one space that their scale shifts up and down.

It's reminiscent of Claes Oldenburg, who's also fascinated by scale. Has he been an influence on you?

Yes a lot. Especially his drawings, his way of seeing things, his humour. But it's clear you can't put a real size lemon into a thousand square metre space.

He was also concerned with dealing with consumerism - is that something that interests you?

Well, I eat a lot of potatoes.

Your depictions of fruit, are, scale aside, quite representational. But the Lemons *you showed at ARC are black, and have a strange device on the side which recalls plastic lemons with their screw tops.*

First of all I travelled across Europe to try to find someone to make these pieces - they were either too heavy or too expensive. Then, I found it was absolutely impossible to find a real lemon that anyone could work from to enlarge. But when I presented a plastic lemon to the marble people in Carrara, they understood immediately, because it's an idealised form. The *Black Lemons* were something like the obverse of the Hollywood Oscars. A gift for bad manners, a black lemon.

Rather than being critiques of consumption these works seemed to offer a sour sort of sustenance?

Well, many people read them as erotic sculptures, finding sexual innuendoes - 'look there's a breast, and there's another one...'

They also look like bombs or mines.

And in a way all those responses are truer to the work than highly intellectualised readings.

Language, punning seems to play a crucial role in your work.

Everything is based on very fast images and very easy words. I see drawing as a language, but one that can be read in different ways.

Why is it that when you use written words in the drawings and the flags they are often English?

As soon as I cross borders I dream in English. I don't really see myself as German. I live in Germany but I travel all the time through Europe. The German and English languages also share certain roots, so through the use of this pidgeon English some basic meanings are revealed.

We've talked about the models, but what about the large sculptures which also seem to relate to architecture?

Many things come from sleepless nights. Sometimes I get up at 5 in the morning, and make a sketch in the dark, before I forget it. While I think about it, design it, decide where to put the screws, the object itself becomes very straightforward - because it doesn't come from making, but from thinking. If these pieces relate to architecture it's just that they are big forms, they need that scale to work. They are like scenery, and the viewer becomes part of the set, something I enjoy because I don't see myself as making individual pieces scattered across a big space. I see a whole room in each piece, with the viewer as actor on stage.

The stage is not only occupied by the viewer, but also by the figures you create. They seem to fall into four categories: silhouetted or cut-out figures; large individual heads; strange three-legged constructions with a head on top; and little toy figures. Do these four representations of the human figure have different functions?

The cut-outs are a way of avoiding having to make 500 individual heads to represent a large crowd of people. The toy figures are there to give a sense of scale only, for photographs of the pieces. They are from *Star Wars*. They're ideal because they are on a scale of 1:20 - architectural figures are too small. This scale is what is used in stage design, in theatre. The figures in the *Laundry* I made myself but I had great trouble with the structure for the arms. There are 50 or 60 of them, black and white, dressed up in my old clothes. I've stopped making figures now, I've run out of characters. But I don't understand why more artists aren't working in this area, there are endless possibilities, and it's so much fun to do.

An important element in both the production of your works, and in their own right are your drawings.

At the root of the drawings is a continuous diary. I draw continuously, and have been doing so for 16 years. It's so easy, so simple and so satisfying because you can do it anywhere, in a park, in the middle of a dinner party. My works don't come from anywhere else but the sketchbook. It's so much fun to express yourself with the minimum of materials, you can make a drawing with a burnt match. I make them like a production line sometimes, 10 or 15 in one day. When the situation between West and East Germany erupted last year, I spent a whole month, 30 days of drawing.

Using a multiplicity of elements you not only create places, whole environments, but you also people them - you seem to create

small worlds, once described as 'theatrum mundi'. Are you interested in the idea of Utopia when you make these nowhere lands?

It's a pity that there's no common idea of Utopia. This notion has completely disappeared - sketches of the future are, in retrospect, only funny. Today everyone is a realist, everybody is pragmatic, especially the art world.

But after the 'no future' mentality of the '80s there seems to be a more optimistic attitude, mirrored perhaps in the progress of your own work, from the more pessimistic mood of the earlier pieces, such as the Museum Crematorium, *to a phase which seems, more open to possibility.*

I see the present in the West as having a big digestion problem. After all this feeding, the consumption of the '80s, there has to be time to digest, to digest even ideas, it's a normal, natural process and it can hurt. And only concern about things around you breaking down doesn't help. We can do basic things. As for optimism and pessimism, this is something for the business section of the newspapers. Parents describe their children as playing - but their games are very serious, like gambling. The fantastic thing is the rules, there is no game without them. You invent them as you play the game, and then you follow them. And if the rules don't work you have to change them. If things don't work in my pieces, I reassemble them, I put this element on top, or turn it around, this is also part of the rules. Even not making, even zero is a part of the game.

The work seems to encompass two states - the brightly coloured Control Boxes *in ARC are also a way of regimenting people; the* Pyramid *is a tomb; the lemons were black and rotting. The works seem to encompass both life and death?*

I can't make explanations for this work, others can make their interpretations. For me this activity is just a way of living and doing things. I have to enjoy them otherwise I can't continue. Sooner or later I will retire. You can't just be a production line of artworks. You need time, for thinking, for preparation. I can also imagine doing nothing...

Interviewed by Iwona Blazwick and Andrea Schlieker, London, 22 September 1990

Alain Colas 1989

Berries 1990

Casino 1990

Pyramid 1986

over:
DEKA flags and *Black Lemons*
installation ARC, Paris 1990

Passtück 1989
coloured aluminium
46 x 50 x 10 cm

Franz West

Zitat 1985
papier maché, metalfoil, wood
212 x 95 x 25 cm

The jagged, almost scatological surfaces of your work, and its relation to the body recall some aspects of Aktionismus. Do you feel your sculpture has some relationship to the work of Rainer, Nitsch and Mühl?

The Aktionismus movement dominated the artistic scene in Austria, and I disliked the idea of being absorbed by it. At the beginning I understood it as a way of life, some kind of an anti-position from the usual position of life... But afterwards it became more like a sect. Everyone was getting some kind of assistance on the fringes of this phenomenon. And I wanted to get out. It seemed rather old and rather boring to me. And in the end, Nitsch is living in his commune outside Vienna, in one of the last enclaves. Aktionismus broke down, and everything became "Disneylanded".

You don't think there is a sensibility in your work of rupturing the boundaries of the body?

Of course there could be a comparison with my work, sometimes when I am making my sculptures, I see them as bones, or as meat. But I am not a member of that school, I'm not a member of that generation. When I decided to start work, I responded to the work of minimal artists. I could only see this in Vienna through photographs. About thirty years ago, it seemed really very new. I didn't see it at the time as a contemplative way of looking at things, like Harald Szeeman does, though now I can see it that way. I just saw it as something really extraordinary, like a street sign pointing in a different direction.

Were you perhaps interested in the theatre of space in minimal work?

Space, space here, space there... I was never really thinking about that. I did not think I would be that kind of an artist. I made some collages in the beginning, and then I moved to sculpture because I wanted something optical but not just in two dimensions, something you could touch, something you could move.

Most minimalist sculpture resists touch and you are saying you wanted a sculpture which would attract touch?

I wanted to touch something that was art. I have been reading a good pseudotheory by Norbert Elias, who wrote about time, and he said that in a universe where nothing moves and you also don't move, you can't have a feeling of time. If everything is absolutely steady, then you are also steady. You couldn't measure time, in fact there wouldn't be time. Measuring time would simply be a social convention. But if you can move something, there would be some real time. During the

moment of Body Art, I made something in Vienna called "Passtück", concave and convex forms, like the devices that are used to prop things up or hang things from. The subjects could move around them, like a do-it-yourself Body Art. The "Passtück" also relates to psychology in a way because it has to do with this inner threshold which you have to cross by involving your body.

You once called them "wearable neuroses"...

If you could see a neurosis, it might look like that. But it's just a slogan, it doesn't really explain the situation if you take it seriously. Nobody would like to show their neurosis like this, as if they were extremities growing out of the body. To ask an artist to show his neurosis as a Body Artist is some kind of realisation of the neurosis of the artist.

Are you inverting the spectacle which the artist presents and making the viewer the spectacle?

Yes I wanted to have the opposite relationship to that of Aktionismus. There's a kind of realism here.

Do you think that when the spectator picks up a "Passtück", engages with it, moulds his or her body to it, that they are liberating themselves from their own constraints?

No, no, the opposite. Nobody normally uses them, or at least only very naïve people. But there is one way to use them, to go beyond a point of inner repression. This is an important point. But it's also a cliché because everyone wants to do that. In the first happenings, the first manifestos, the people who came were always involved in doing something. But then it was divided, like a theatre, it was called a performance. There was a stage where the artist was and it was like a theatre. But I wanted to pass this point where you were relegated to the outside, and pass to the inside of the artwork. "Passtück" implies to adapt but also to pass, a system of transition. I want the art work to be real, not like a dream or a movie, but to be able to step into it, to sit on it, lie on it.

Can we talk about some of these works on plinths, the papier-maché works? Why are their surfaces so rough, even expressionistic? Ulrich Loock described them as almost like a digestive system, with mouths and orifices.

I don't know why they got like this. The paper is a very cheap material and very good to work with. You put newspaper in and you mix it up and it becomes very fine, like a cream or a hair shampoo. I made some things with polyester, but then you have to have rubber and good shoes and a mask.

Is working with your hands important?

It's a very usual thing.

It's an anti-technological approach?

Absolutely, it's working in nature. They are studies next to nature. Next to nature is the newspaper, in it you see the world, the everyday world.

Often you put papier-maché around a bottle or a broom.

They are just souvenirs. I didn't like all the more technological, machine-made, very precise sculptures. So I took something that is made very precisely on a machine and covered it.

The scale of the works is rarely large?

In the beginning I worked in a small room. Even now I work in a small room. Maybe this is a tradition in Vienna, all the rooms are small. So some of the works can be as large as rooms. In a way, it's a conventional way of making forms, it's more classical, like conventional sculpture, in Giacometti or Moore for example. Not like the way Jeff Koons makes something in bronze. It's almost become taboo to make forms by yourself. The idea now is that you should not make any forms.

Do you mean invent forms, rather than use forms that already exist?

Yes, I see no biological reason not to.

Perhaps there is a marriage between a Duchampian tradition in your work and an Expressionist one?

If I wanted to make a ready-made today, I would make the pissoir, but one you could really piss into, in a museum. Recently I made something for the kitchen, a sieve, but you can use it, and then put it back on the plinth. And a shopping bag, with a very beautiful design... It's about searching for the art, somewhere between the artist and the technician.

The sculptures try and find their way back to their maker?

The missing object is the breast of your mother, like Lacan said, though in a more complicated language. It's always the same problem, of concave and convex. This is partially the concern of the "Passtück", but if you say it, you risk losing it.

When you are at your mother's breast, you don't have any sense of the boundaries of your body. You are a boundless entity, and when you grow up, the boundaries of your body are a sort of civilisation.

It goes away, it doesn't do what you want, it isn't always here when you want it... to be parted is a problem. Perhaps these are parted objects.

So there is an equivalent here between the child learning that he or she has become autonomous, and no longer so reliant on the mother, and the sculpture which has to be autonomous but wants the spectator.

Yes, yes, and when the spectator is autonomous he says he doesn't want to touch this really.

You get the feeling looking at your works that they are unhygienic.

Yes, I don't like this hygienic quality, it's very sterile. Also, they become dirty when they are used, they were white and they become grey and dirty, biological and living.

Why did you then choose to use colour?

It's important to escape any programme, any strict programme. It's like listening to music or having music in the background. First I liked modern music, modern beat, the Beatles etc., and then I wanted to disturb my programme of listening to this music. After a few years the forms had become very classical. Now I like listening to noise music, very anti-bourgeois music, very loud in a room. Colour is usually associated with something more pejorative, a sign of naïvety or illusionism. But the colour is very hard to operate, I was afraid to use it. So I was sitting in the studio of Herbert Brandl, and as he is a painter, I asked him to paint the sculptures. This was my first collaboration.

Your furniture seems to relate to modernist design or architecture?

I was interested in architecture to start with. I studied at a school of architecture but they threw me out. I thought that with architecture you could solve some problems. My furniture is quite discrete, quite minimal.

Everything you have said points to a version of the Gesamtkunstwerk, to do with living, eating in a space, with art somehow in the middle of this.

Well, there's a tradition of this in Vienna. Don Judd said that a chair and a work of art are completely different. My understanding is that it is absolutely not different. If I make a chair, I say it's an artwork.

At the same time, you use the plinth.

There was a convention in modern sculpture, no more plinths, Minimalism insisted on there being no plinths anymore.

So was this a reaction against Minimalism?

No, no, a reaction against rules.

Even the chairs are on a plinth.

Yes, and you can get on to the plinth yourself.The artist lives in a social environment, he doesn't just produce work from the other side. I made this exhibition in Vienna, in the Kunsthistorisches Museum, with all these chairs and couches. And some people sat there, harmless people, and I also would go and sit there. And if you can forget everything, put the ugliness away, then maybe this is a place for art... this is the art of today, lying down on the bed looking up into space. It doesn't matter what the art looks like but how it's used. The important thing is to find a place for art, not a description.

The process of collaboration is important to you?

This democratic idea of artists working alongside each other is important to me. I made all these chairs with some young aristocrats in Vienna, who came to me and wanted to do some welding. In the Bible there is the imperative that you have to earn your daily bread with the sweat of your brow, and maybe these aristocrats wanted to earn their daily living by sweating (note: the German word for sweating is very close to the word for welding). A sort of "Paradise Lost". It's very strange, because these aristocrats welded the chairs, they rendered the process inimitable. All the furniture, every single chair or couch was made by them. I can't make the chairs again because I'm not an aristocrat. Originally I felt they were designed, now I know that they are not. The sculptures are a kind of noble design.

Why is that of importance, who made the chair?

It's just a situation, that's all. If you want to have one of these chairs, maybe you can find an aristocrat but they don't usually weld. Now the situation for collaborating is a little more difficult because of the market situation. It changes your life absolutely, this socio-economic system.

Eo Ipso seems half-way between a "Passtück" and a piece of furniture. It's made from an old washing machine.

It was the washing machine of my mother, who had died. I used this because the sculpture was for outside, in Münster. Normally I'm not interested in making sculpture with metal, and I didn't know how to make this sculpture for outside. And then they introduced this aristocrat to me. He was making something for the gallery, some chairs. And some new forms came from this collaboration.

Although at the beginning of the discussion you said that everything had become "Disneylanded", do you think that there is a new sense of hope around, a more positive attitude?

Now you can ignore the Disneyland. It's not so much to do with a new sense of hope, it's more that everyday life has returned.

Interviewed by Iwona Blazwick, James Lingwood and Andrea Schlieker, London, 15 September 1990

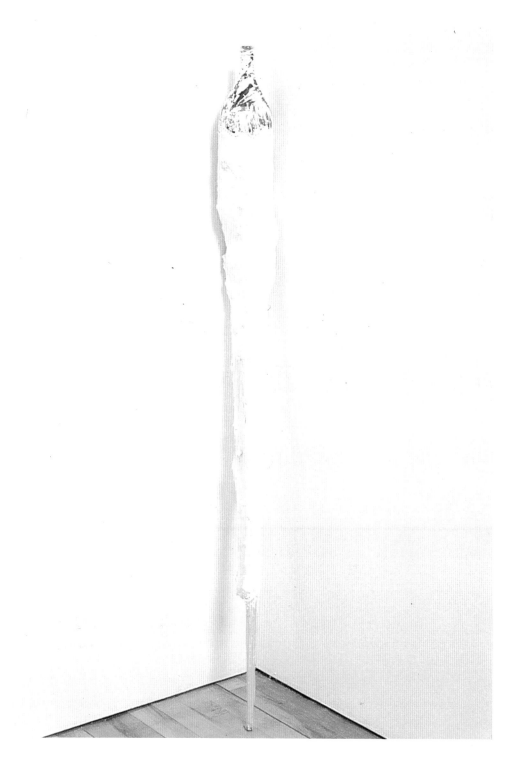

Untitled 1988
glass, wood, plaster
138 x 14 x 14 cm

Untitled 1990
painted papier maché, plastic
37 x 55 x 33 cm

Installation Kunsthistorisches Museum, Vienna 1989/90

Eo Ipso 1987
metal
118 x 546 x 115 cm; 83 x 57 x 52 cm
made in collaboration with Mathis Esterhazy

Biographies

Miroslaw Balka

Born in 1958 Warsaw, Poland
Lives and works in Otwock, Poland

SOLO EXHIBITIONS
1985
Wilki - Niewilki, TSPP, Warsaw
1986
Precepta Patris Mei Servivi Semper, Pokaz Gallery, Warsaw
1989
River, Labiyrnt Gallery, Lublin
Installation - Abel, PO Gallery, Zielona Gora
1990
Good God, Dziekanka Gallery, Warsaw

SELECTED GROUP EXHIBITIONS
1986
Figures and Objects, BWA Gallery, Pulawy
Expressions of the '80s, BWA Gallery, Sopot
1987
II Biennale of New Art, Zielona Gora
Co Slychac, Zaklady Norblin, Warsaw
1988
Sculpture in the Garden, SARP, Warsaw
B.K.K., Haag Centrum Voor Aktuele Kunst, Den Haag
Polish Realities, Third Eye Centre, Glasgow
1989
Feelings, Dziekanka, Warsaw
Lochy Manhattanu, Filmmuseum, Lodz
Middle Europe, Artists Space, New York
Dialog, Kunstmuseum Düsseldorf
1990
Aperto, XIII Venice Biennale

SELECTED BIBLIOGRAPHY
1987
Anda Rottenberg, *Draught*, Nike, No.2
1990
Maria Morzuch, *Persistance*, Oko i ucho, No.I
Joanna Kiliszek, Interview, Flash Art

CATALOGUES
1987
What's Going On, Norblin Factory, Warsaw
1988
Anda Rottenberg, B.K.K., Haag Centrum Voor Aktuele Kunst, Den Haag
Maria Morzuch, *Polish Realities*, Third Eye Centre, Glasgow
1989
Maria Morzuch, *Dialog*, Kunstmuseum Düsseldorf/Centre of Contemporary Art, Warsaw
Valerie Smith, *Metaphysical Visions/Middle Europe*, Artists Space, New York
1990
Joanna Kiliszek, *Good God*, Galeria Dziekanka, Warsaw
Aperto, XIII Venice Biennale

Stephan Balkenhol

Born 1957 in Fritzlar/Hessen

SOLO EXHIBITIONS
1984/88
Galerie Löhrl, Mönchengladbach
1985
A.O.Kunstraum, Hamburg
Kunstverein Bochum
1987
Kunstverein Braunschweig
1987/90
Deweer Art Gallery, Zwevegem-Otegem/Belgium
1988
Kunsthalle Basel
Galerie Johnen & Schöttle, Cologne
Portikus, Frankfurt
1989
Kunsthalle, Nurenberg
Galerie Rüdiger Schöttle, Munich
Galerie Mai 36, Luzern

GROUP EXHIBITIONS
1983
Impulse 1, Galerie Löhrl, Mönchengladbach
1984
Die Stipendiaten der Karl-Schmidt-Rottluff-Stiftung,
Brücke Museum, Berlin
Es ist wie es ist, Kunstverein für die Rheinlande und Westfalen,
Düsseldorf
1985
Ausstellungshallen Mathildenhöhe, Darmstadt
Skulptur in Hamburg, Landesvertretung Hamburg in Bonn
1986
Jenisch-Park, Skulpturenausstellung in Hamburg
Momente - Zum Thema Urbanität, Kunstverein Braunschweig
S.Balkenhol, L.Gerdes, E.Karnauke, Kasseler Kunstverein
1987
Neue Kunst in Hamburg, Kampnagelfabrik, Hamburg
A Choice, Contemporary art from Europe, RAI Amsterdam
Galerie Johnen & Schöttle, Cologne

Skulptur Projekte, Münster
Theatergarten Bestiarium, Munich
Exotische Welten, Europäische Phantasien, Württembergischer,
Kunstverein, Stuttgart
1988
Bi-Nationale, Kunsthalle Düsseldorf and ICA Boston
Rüdiger Schöttle, Munich
Dorothea v.Stetten-Preis, Kunstmuseum Bonn
1989
Prospekt '89, Frankfurt

SELECTED BIBLIOGRAPHY
1987
Jürgen Schmidt-Missner, *Ein Stern geht auf*, Harburger Anzeiger,
No10, February
Peter Winte, *Baum-Menschen*, Frankfurter Allgemeine Zeitung,
10 March
1988
Sabine B.Vogel, *Querblicke*, Wolkenkratzer Art Journal, No 8
1989
Dieter Koepplin, *Stephan Balkenhol*, Parkett, No.22
Anna Brenken, *Stephan Balkenhol, Bildhauer*, ART, No 1, January
Konstanze Crüwell-Doertenbach, *Stephan Balkenhol*, Nike, No 27,
April
Gregorio Magnani, *This is not Conceptual Art*, Flash Art, No 145,
March/April

CATALOGUES
1985
Ulrich Rückriem, *Stephan Balkenhol - Skulpturen*, Ausstellungshallen
Mathildenhöhe, Darmstadt
Irmgard Gercke, *Bilder vom Menschen im Werk von Gerhard Richter
und Stephan Balkenhol*, Katalog Neue Galerie, Sammlung Ludwig,
Aachen
1986
Bernd Ernsting, *Zu Stephan Balkenhols Reiter*, Jenisch-Park; Skulptur,
von der Kulturbehörde Hamburg

1987

Suzanne Weirich, *Stephan Balkenhol - Mann mit grünem Hemd und weisser Hose*, Skulptur Projekte, Münster/Cologne

Wilhelm Bojescul, *Anmerkungen zur Arbeit von Stephan Balkenhol*, Kunstverein Braunschweig

Günter Gercken, *Menschenbilder von Stephan Balkenhol*, Katalog Neue Kunst in Hamburg 1987, Hamburg

Ludger Gerdes, *Balkenhols Standbilder*, **Stephan Balkenhol**, Kunstverein Braunschweig

1988

Jeff Wall, *Bezugspunkte im Werk von Stephan Balkenhol*, Stephan Balkenhol, Kunsthalle Basel

Jean-Christophe Amman, *Stephan Balkenhol*, Kunsthalle Basel

Rainer Crone, *Stephan Balkenhol* (interview), Jürgen Harten, David A Ross, Deutsche Kunst der späten 80er Jahre, Städtische Kunsthalle und Kunstammlung Nordrhein-Westfalen, Düsseldorf

Dieter Koepplin, *Stephan Balkenhol*, Dorothea v. Stetten-Kunstpreis, Städtisches Kunstmuseum Bonn

1989

Gregorie Magnani, *Sei Artisti Tedeschi*, Castello di Rivara, Turin

1990

Stephan Balkenhol, *Zeichnungen und Entwürfe für Skulpturen 1990*, Deweer Art Gallery, Otegem, Belgium

Jean-Marc Bustamante

Born in 1952 Toulouse
Lives and works in Paris

SELECTED SOLO EXHIBITIONS
1982
Galerie Badoin Lebon, Paris
1984
Galerie Crousel Hussenot, Paris
1986
Galerie Bärbel Grässlin, Frankfurt
Galerie Philip Nelson, Villeurbanne
Musée St Pierre, Lyon
1987
Galerie Micheline Szwajcer, Antwerp
1988
Galerie Ghislaine Hussenot, Paris
1989
Galerie Joost Declercq, Ghent
Kunsthalle Bern
1990
Museum Haus Lange, Krefeld

SELECTED GROUP EXHIBITIONS
1980
Biennale de Paris
1982
Musée Cantini, Marseille
1985
Rendez-vous, Lothringerstrasse, Munich
Les seconds Ateliers de Fontevraud
Alles und noch viel mehr, Kunsthalle Bern
Biennale Graz
12 artistes dans l'espace, Seibu Museum, Tokyo
1986
Aperto, XIII Venice Biennale
Een Kreuze R.A.I., Amsterdam
Centre d'Art Contemporain, Geneva
7th Sydney Biennial
Sonsbeek 86, Arnheim
A Distanced View, The New Museum of Contemporary Art, New York

1987
l'époque, la mode, la morale, la passion, Centre Georges Pompidou, Paris
Documenta 8, Kassel

SELECTED BIBLIOGRAPHY
1987
Jean François Chevrier, *The things that go bump*, Artforum, October
1988
Jerome Sans, *Jean-Marc Bustamante*, Flash Art, summer
1989
Jerome Sans, *Jean-Marc Bustamante*, Artforum, May
Tony Godfrey, *Report from Paris 1*, Art in America, October
1990
Jean François Chevrier, *Jean-Marc Bustamante. Le Lieu de l'Art*, Galeries Magazine, Feb-March
Rob Perree, Kunstbeeld, April
Renee Steenbergen, *Galerie. Bustamante*, Handelsblad, 23 March
Piet Je.Tegenbosch, *Stichting De Appel. Jean-Marc Bustamante*, De Volkskrant, 24 March
H.J. Ingenpahs, *Objekte schaffen einen seltsamen Ort*, Westdeutsche Zeitung, 27 January
H.J. Ingenpahs, *Das heimliche Spiel mit Hülle und Kern*, Westdeutsche Zeitung, 7 February
Pascaline Cuvelier, *L'un Schütte, l'autre Bustamante*, Liberation, June

CATALOGUES
1989
Ulrich Loock & Alain Cueff, *Bustamante*, Kunsthalle Bern
1990
Julian Heynen, *Jean-Marc Bustamante*, Museum Haus Lange, Krefeld
Suzanne Pagé & Alain Cueff, *Jean-Marc Bustamante*, ARC/Musée d'Art Moderne de la Ville de Paris

Asta Gröting

Born 1961 in Herford
Lives and works in Düsseldorf

SOLO EXHIBITIONS
1988
Galerie Isabella Kacprzak, Stuttgart
Galerie Sophia Ungers, Cologne
1989
Kunstverein für die Rheinlande und Westfalen, Düsseldorf
1989/90
Galerie Isabella Kacprzak, Cologne

GROUP EXHIBITIONS
1985
Lothringer Strasse, Munich
1990
The Readymade Boomerang, 8th Sydney Biennial
Aperto, XIII Venice Biennale
A.-und W.Grohmann Stipendium, Baden-Baden

SELECTED BIBLIOGRAPHY
1988
Jutta Koether, *Asta Gröting, Galerie Ungers*, Artforum, October
Isabelle Graw, *Asta Gröting, Galerie Ungers*, Flash Art, October
1989
Renate Puvogel, *Asta Gröting, Galerie Kacprzak*, Kunstforum, July/ August
Noemi Smolik, *Asta Gröting, Kunstverein Düsseldorf*, Noema 27, November
Norbert Messler, *Asta Gröting, Galerie Kacprzak*, Artscribe, November
1990
Norbert Messler, *Asta Gröting, Kunstverein Düsseldorf*, Artform, January

CATALOGUES
1989
Jiri Svestka, Kunstverein für die Rheinlande und Westfalen, Düsseldorf. Galerie Isabella Kacprzak, Cologne
1990
Gudrun Inboden, *Das Geheimnis des Offenen in der Kunst Asta Grötings*, Kunsthalle Baden-Baden
Art is Easy, 8th Sydney Biennial

Juan Muñoz

Born 1953, Madrid
Lives and works in Madrid

SOLO EXHIBITIONS
1984
Ultimos Trabajos, Galeria Fernando Vijande, Madrid
1985
Galeria Comicos, Lisbon
1986/89
Galerie Joost Declercq, Ghent
1987
Sculpture de 1985 à 1987, Musée d'Art Contemporain, Bordeaux
1987
Galerie Roger Pailhas, Marseilles
1987/89
Lisson Gallery, London
1987/89
Galeria Marga Paz, Madrid
1987-88
Estudos para a descricao de um lugar, Galeria Comicos, Lisbon
1988
Galeria Jean Bernier, Athens
Galerie Konrad Fischer, Düsseldorf
Galerie Ghislaine Hussenot, Paris
1990
Arnolfini, Bristol

SELECTED GROUP EXHIBITIONS
1981
Friart, Fribourg
Room 202, PSI, New York
1982
Büro Berlin, Berlin
1983
Seis Españoles en Madrid, Galeria Fernando Vijande, Madrid
La Imagen del Animal, Caja de Ahorros, Madrid
1985
V Salon de los 16, Museo Español de Arte Contemporaneo, Madrid
Stedelijk Van Abbemuseum, Eindhoven
1986
Caja de Pensiones, Madrid

Aperto, XII Venice Biennale
Ateliers Internationaux des Pays de la Loire, Fondation Nationale des Arts Graphiques et Plastiques, Abbaye de Fontevraud
1987
Dynamiques et Interrogations, ARC, Paris
1989
Theatergarden Bestiarium, PSI, New York
Magiciens de la Terre, Centre Georges Pompidou & La Grande Halle, Paris
Presencias e Procesos, Casa da Parra, Santiago de Compostela
Spanish Art Today, The Museum of Modern Art, Takanawa, Tokyo
Psychological Abstraction, Deste Foundation at The House of Cyprus, Athens
1990
OBJECTives: the New Sculpture, Newport Harbour Art Museum, California
A Group Show, Marian Goodman Gallery, New York

SELECTED BIBLIOGRAPHY
1984
Francisco Calvo Serraller, *La Tercera Mirada del Misterio, Juan Muñoz*, El Päis, 17 November
1985
Gloria Collado, *70,80,90... La Historia Interminable -Rumbo a lo Desconocido*, Lapiz, February
Joao Pinharda, *Retrato de una Epoca*, Mais, 15 March
Alexandre Melo, *O Jogo e Entre a Consciencia e a Impossibilidade*, Journal de Letras, 19 March
1986
Jutta Koether & Diedrich Diederichsen, *Jutta and Diedrich go to Spain: Spanish Art and Culture viewed from Madrid*, Artscribe, Sep-Oct
Pier Luigi Tazzi, *Albrecht Dürer would have come too*, Artforum, September
Francisco Calvo Serraller, *Las Imagenes rotas de un Agonista*, El Päis, 19 December
1987
Gloria Collado, *Tierra Desierta*, Guia del Ocio, January
Jose Ramon Danvila, *Contra Todo Tipe de Circunstancias*, El Punto, December-January
José-Luis Brea, *Juan Muñoz: Nada es tan opaco como un espejo*, Sur Expres, April-May

Kevin Power, *Juan Muñoz*, Artscribe, Summer 1988

José-Luis Brea, *Juan Muñoz. The Other speaks*, New Art International

Michael Phillipson, *Juan Muñoz*, Artscribe, March/April

José-Luis Brea, *Juan Muñoz . The System of Objects*, Flash Art, January-February

Carolyn Christov-Bakargiev, *Something Nowhere*, Flash Art, May-June

Luk Lambrecht, *Juan Muñoz . Joost Declercq, Ghent*, Flash Art, October

1989

Catherine Grout, *Cristina Iglesias, Juan Muñoz: sculptures*, Artstudio, Autumn

Jeffrey Deitch, *Psychological Abstraction*, Flash Art, November-December

J.M.Costa, *Juan Muñoz: la temperancia del objeto*, El Punto, 21 April

Alexandre Melo, *That cannot be said any other way*, Artforum, May

1990

Tim Marlow, *Juan Muñoz*, The Burlington Magazine, February

Aurora Garcia, *Juan Muñoz*, Artforum, February

James Roberts, *Juan Muñoz*, Artefactum, February-March

CATALOGUES AND BOOKS

1983

Seis Españoles en Madrid, Galeria Fernando Vijande, Madrid

Joseph Beuys, Ramon Bilbao, Julio Caro-Baroja, Manuel Martin-Bueno, Mario Merz, Juan Muñoz, Eduardo Ripoll-Perello, *La Imagen del Animal*, Caja de Ahorros, Madrid and La Caixa de Barcelona

1984

Jan Debbaut, *Juan Muñoz. Ultimos Trabajos*, Galeria Fernando Vijande, Madrid

1985

Jan Debbaut & Rudi Fuchs, C.Dichgans, L.Dujourie, M.Dumas, L.Foxcroft, K.de Goede, F.Van Hemert, C.Iglesias, H.Klingelhöller, M.Luyten, J.Muñoz, K.Porter, J.Sarmento, B.Schmidt-Heins, G.Schmidt-Heins, D.Vermeiren, Stedelijk Van Abbemuseum, Eindhoven

1986

Jan Hoet, *Chambre d'Amis*, Museum Van Hedendaagse Kunst, Ghent

Kevin Power, *1981-1986. Pintores y Escultores Españoles*, Fundación Caja de Pensiones, Madrid

1987

Jean Marc Poinsot & Juan Muñoz, *Juan Muñoz. Sculptures de 1985 à 1987*, Musée d'art Contemporain, Bordeaux

José-Luis Brea, *Lili Dujouris/Juan Muñoz*, FRAC des Pays de La Loire, Abbaye de Fontevraud

1989

Jeffrey Deitch, *Psychological Abstraction*, Deste Foundation for Contemporary Art

Spanish Art Today, The Museum of Modern Art, Takanawa, Tokyo

Magiciens de la Terre, Centre Georges Pompidou, Paris

1990

Lucinda Barnes, *OBJECTives : The New Sculpture*, Newport Harbour Art Museum, California

TEXTS BY THE ARTIST

1983

Correspondencias in 5 Arquitectos, 5 Escultores, Caja de Ahorros, Madrid (ex cat)

Los Primeros - Los Ultimos, La Imagen del Animal, Caja de Ahorros, Madrid and La Caixa de Barcelona (ex cat)

1985

The Best Sculpture is a Toy Horse, Domus, No 659, March

La palabra como escultura, Figura, No 4, winter

1986

Desde . . . a . . . , Figura, No 5, spring

De la luminosa oppacidad de los signos, Figura, No 6, autumn

El Hijo Mayor de Laooconte, Chema Cobo, Kunstmuseum Bern (ex cat)

Un hombre subido a una farola, Escultura Inglesa entre el Objeto y la Imagen, Palacio de Velasquez, Madrid (ex cat)

1989

Tres Imagenes o Cuatro, Art Today, Museum of Modern Art, Takanawa, Tokyo (ex cat)

Thomas Schütte

Born 1954 in Oldenburg
Lives and works in Dusseldorf

SOLO EXHIBITIONS
1980/82/86
Galerie Rüdiger Schöttle, Munich
1981/85/87/89/90
Galerie Konrad Fischer, Düsseldorf
1983
Galerie Konrad Fischer, Zurich
1984/85/86/89/90
Galerie Philip Nelson, Lyon
1984/85
Produzentengalerie, Hamburg
1984
Galerie Johnen & Schöttle, Cologne
1984/87
Galerie Jean Bernier, Athens
1985/87
Galerie Micheline Szwajcer, Antwerp
1986
Galerie Crousel-Hussenot, Paris
Museum Haus Lange, Krefeld
1986/88
Galerie Tucci Russo, Turin
1987
Lichthof Landesmuseum, Munich
Museum Overholland, Amsterdam
1988
Galerie Christian Stein, Milan
Staatliche Kunsthalle, Baden-Baden
1989
Musée de Clamecy, Clamecy
Portikus, Frankfurt
Stichting de Appel, Amsterdam
Pietro Sparta, Chagny
Ute Parduhn, Düsseldorf
1989/90
Marian Goodman Gallery, New York
1990
Kunsthalle, Bern

ARC, Paris
Van Abbe Museum, Eindhoven
Crousel Bama, Paris

SELECTED GROUP EXHIBITIONS
1981
Art Allemagne Aujourd'hui, Musée d'Art Moderne, Paris
Westkunst, Messehallen, Cologne
1983
Standort Düsseldorf, Kunsthalle Düsseldorf
Rekonstruktion, Städtische Galerie, Regensburg
Sculpture From Germany, San Francisco - New York
1984
Der versiegelte Brunnen, Kunststichting, Rotterdam
Museum Haus Esters, Krefeld
Kunstlandschaft BRD, Kunstverein Freiburg
von hier aus, Messegelände (Halle 13), Düsseldorf
Octobre des Arts, Musée St.Pierre, Lyon
Im Mittelpunkt : Kunsthalle Münsterland, Münster
Ouverture, Castello di Rivoli, Turin
1985
The European Iceberg, Art Gallery of Ontario, Toronto
Nouvelle Biennale, parc de la Villette, Paris
Rheingold, Palazzo Promotrice, Turin
Sonsbeek 86, Arnheim
1945-1985, Nationalgalerie, Berlin
1986
Sieben Skulpturen, Kunstverein Cologne
Origins and Beyond, 6th Sydney Biennial
Correspondentie Europa, Stedelijk Museum, Amsterdam
Sie machen was sie wollen, Galerie Schipka, Sofia
1987
Tekennen'87, Kunststichting, Rotterdam
Raumbilder, Reina Sofia, Madrid
Juxtapositions, P. S .1, New York
Im Auftrag, Museum Museum Folkwang, Essen
l'époque . . . la passion, Centre Georges Pompidou, Paris
Documenta 8, Kassel
Skulptur-Projekte, Landesmuseum und Stadt, Münster
das andere Medium, Museum am Ostwall, Dortmund
Musée St. Pierre, Kunstverein Frankfurt

Hacen io que quieren, Museo de Arte Contemporanea, Seville

1988

L' inventaire, Manufrance, St . Etienne

1989

Skulpturen für Krefeld, Museum Haus Esters, Krefeld

Zeitzeichen, Museum der Bildenden Künste, Leipzig

Blickpunkte, Musée d'Art Contemporain, Montreal

1990

Musée d'Art Moderne de la Ville de Paris

Stedelijk van Abbemuseum, Eindhoven

SELECTED BIBLIOGRAPHY

1983

Ulrich Loock, *Sculpture ou mise en condition? Aspects of a problem*,
Artists No 14 January/February

Jörg Johnen, *Ich lebe hier in Deutschland und muss mich dazu stellen*
(interview with Thomas Schütte, Ludger Gerdes, Michael von Ofen),
Badische Zeitung No 15/16

1985

Martin Hentschel, *Vergessen Macht Glücklich. Ein Gespräch mit
Thomas Schütte*, **NIKE**, January/February No 6

Patrick Javault, *Les états du lieu, Klingelhöller, Luy, Mucha, Schütte*,
Art Press, March No 90

Renate Puvogel, *Pflicht und Kür. Denk-Modelle zwischen Skulptur und
Architektur*, **Das Kunstwerk**, December

1986

Martin Hentschel, *Thomas Schütte im Museum Hans Lange. Die
Wirklichkeit des Möglichen*, **NIKE**, March/April N°12

Ludwig Locker, *Architektonische Aspekte in der Düsseldorfer
Gegenwartskunst*, **Artefactum**, December

1987

Pier Luigi Tazzi, *Thomas Schütte*, **Artforum**, February

1989

Mathilde Roskam, *Performing Poet*, De Appel

1990

Oscarine Bosquet, *Le théâtre de l'oeil*, **Galleries Magazine**, April

CATALOGUES

1983

Thomas Schütte : Lieber Jean Hubert Martin!, *Konstruierte Orte .
6 x D + 1 x NY*, Kunsthalle Bern

Ulrich Loock, Gerdes, Klingelhöller, Luy, Mucha, Schütte, Konrad
Fischer, Düsseldorf

1984

Denys Zacharopoulos & Jean Hubert Martin, Fifteen Monuments by
Thomas Schütte, Galerie Philip Nelson

Ludger Gerdes, Modelle, *von hier aus*, Cologne

1985

Ulrich Loock, Dispositif Sculpture, Interview with Thomas Schütte
ARC, Paris

Martin Hentschel, Ein Gespräch mit Thomas Schütte, *Rheingold*, 40
Künstler aus Cologne and Düsseldorf, Cologne

1986

Ulrich Loock, Wenn . . . , *Pläne I-XXX , 1981*, and
Lazlo Glozer, Vision und Emblem in den Plänen von Thomas Schütte,
Pläne I-XXX, 1981, Produzentengalerie Hamburg

Ulrich Wilmes, *Correspondentie Europa*, Stedelijk Museum, Amsterdam

Julian Heynen, *Thomas Schütte*, Museum Hans Lange, Krefeld

1987

Ulrich Wilmes, Bildlichkeit und Monumentalität, *Obst und Gemüse*,
Projekt für Münster, Westfälisches Landesmuseum Münster

Ulrich Loock, Thomas Schütte, *Aquarellen*, Museum Overholland,
Amsterdam

Martin Hentschel, Schüttes *Eis, Documenta 8*, Kassel

1988

Martin Hentschel, *Für Aussen. Zehn grosse Stücke*,
Kunsthalle Baden-Baden

1989

Julian Heynen, Thomas Schütte. Projekt für denTrockenhof von Haus
Esters, *Skulpturen für Krefeld*, Museum Haus Esters, Krefeld

Kasper König & Saskia Bos, *The Laundry. Mohr's Life*, Portikus,
Frankfurt/M and de Appel, Amsterdam

1990

T.S. : September Notes, Marian Goodman Gallery, New York

Franz West

Born 1947 in Vienna
Lives and works in Vienna

SELECTED SOLO EXHIBITIONS
1980
Galerie nächst St.Stephan, Vienna
1984
Im Klapperhof, Cologne
1985
Kunstzentrum der Engelhorn Stiftung, Munich
Kunsthandlung Hummel, Vienna
1986
Neue Galerie am Landesmuseum Joanneum, Graz
Galerie Max Hetzler, Cologne
Galerie Christoph Dürr, Munich
1986/88
Galerie Peter Pakesch, Vienna 1987
Ansicht, Secession, Vienna 1988
Kunsthalle Bern
Galerie Giorgio Persano, Turin
Galerie Isabella Kacprzak, Stuttgart
Schöne Aussicht, Portikus, Frankfurt
Wegener Räume, Galerie Peter Pakesch, Vienna
1989
Krefelder Kunstmuseum, Museum Haus Lange, Krefeld
P.S.I. Museum, New York
Galerie Gisela Capitain, Cologne

SELECTED GROUP EXHIBITIONS
1981
Westkunst, Cologne
1984
Biennale für Kleinplastik, Budapest
1985/86
Spuren, Skulpturen und Monumente ihrer präzisen Reise, Kunsthaus
Zurich
1986
De Sculptura, Messepalast Wien, Vienna
Sonsbeek '86, Arnheim
Zurück zur Farbe, Budapest

Die Wahlverwandtschaften Zitate, Grazer Kunstverein, Stadtmuseum,
Graz
Skulptur - sein, Kunsthalle Düsseldorf
1987
Skulptur Projekt Münster, Westfälisches Landesmuseum, Münster
Aktuelle Kunst in Östereich, Europalia, Museum van Hedendaagse
Kunst, Ghent
1988
Körper, Kunsthandlung Hummel, Vienna
Aperto, XIII Venice Biennale
Zeitlos, Berlin, Hamburger Bahnhof
Skulpturen Republik, Vienna Messepalast; John Hansard Gallery,
Southampton; Third Eye Centre, Glasgow
1989
Open Mind, Museum van Hedendaagse Kunst, Ghent
Wittgenstein, Secession, Vienna and Sigmund Freud Haus, Vienna

SELECTED BIBLIOGRAPHY
1986
Franz West, Ferdinand Schmatz, Peter Pakesch, *Aus einem Gespräch,
Wien, November 1985*, **Domus** 668, January
Annelie Pohlen, *Franz West*, **Kunstforum** No 85, September/October
Horst Christoph, *Antwort an die schönen Töchter*, **Profil** No 43,
October
Peter Mahr, *Franz West at Peter Pakesch*, **Artscribe** January/February
Helmut Draxler, *Franz West-Plastiker der Psyche*, **Kunst und Kirche**
January
Martin Prinzhorn, August Ruhs, Franz West, Reinhard Priessnitz and
Ferdinand Schmartz, *Franz West*, **Kunstforum**, May/June
Christian Janecke, *Franz West*, **Vernissage**, October
1989
Harald Szeemann, *Franz West ou le baroque de l'ame et de l'esprit en
fragments sèches*, **artpress**, February
Helmuth Draxler, *Franz West : The anti-body to anti-body*, **Artforum**,
March
1990
Brigitte Felderer and Herbert Lachmayer, *Potentially Inaccessible,
Factually Accessible*, **Parkett** No 24

CATALOGUES
1981
Franz West and Reinhard Priessnitz, *Heute*, Museum der Stadt, Cologne
1982
Patrick Frey and Helmut Draxler, *Neue Skulptur. Wien*, Galerie nachst St.Stephan, Vienna
1985
Franz West and Reinhard Priessnitz, *Franz West. München. Engelhorn Stiftung zur Förderung bildender Kunst*, Kunsthandlung Julius Hummel

Weltpunkt Wien. Un regard sur Vienne. 1985, Vienna/Munich, Locker Verlag

Franz West and Ferdinand Schmatz, *Spuren, Skulpturen und Monumente ihrer präzisen Reise*, Kunsthaus Zurich
1986
Franz West, Ferdinand Schmatz, Peter Pakesch, Wilfried Skreiner, *Franz West. Legitime Skulptur*, Graz, Neue Galerie am Landesmuseum Joanneum

Harald Szeemann, *De Sculptura*, Wiener Festwochen, Messepalast

Wilfred Skreiner, *Zurück zur Farbe*, Budapest

Saskia Bos, Antje von Graeventiz and Marianne Brouwer *Sonsbeek '86*, Arnheim

Peter Pakesch, *Die Wahlverwandtschaften-Zitate. Steirischer Herbst '86*, Kunstverein-Stadtmuseum

Skulptur-sein, Kunsthalle Düsseldorf
1987
Peter Pakesch, Ferdinand Schmatz, Heimo Zobernig and Georg Schollhammer and Franz West, *Franz West-Heimo Zobernig*, Galerie Christoph Dürr, Munich

Julian Heynen, *Anderer Leute Kunst*, Museum Haus Lange, Krefeld

Jan Hoet and Bart De Baere, *Actuelle Kunst in Osternijk*, Museum van Hedendaagse Kunst, Ghent

Brandl - West, Galerie Giorgio Persano, Turin

Kasper König, *Franz West. Schöne Aussicht*, Portikus, Frankfurt

Harald Szeemann, *Zeitlos*, Hamburger Bahnhof, Berlin
1988
Pier Luigi Tazzi, Fotos Balthazar Burkhard, *Fontana Romana*, Edizione Pieroni, Rome

1989
Julian Heynen, Ferdinand Schmatz, Franz West, Museum Haus Lange, Krefeld (with photographs by Günther Förg)

Joseph Kosuth, *Wittgenstein, Das Spiel des Unsagbaren*, Wiener Secession
1990
Hans Hollein, Enrico Comi, *Franz West*, Austrian Pavilion, XIII Venice Biennale

Lenders

Österreichisches Museum für angewandte Kunst, Vienna

Jean Bernier Gallery, Athens

Galerie Crousel-Robelin-BAMA, Paris

Galerie Luc Declercq, Knokke-Heist

Deweer Art Gallery, Otegem

Galerie Konrad Fischer, Düsseldorf

Collection Herbert, Ghent

Galerie Ghislaine Hussenot, Paris

Galerie Johnen & Schöttle, Cologne

Galerie Isabella Kacprzak, Cologne

Galerie Löhrl, Mönchengladbach

Collection Ludwig, Aachen

Galerie Peter Pakesch, Vienna

Stedelijk Van Abbemuseum, Eindhoven

Collection Ryszard Varisella, Frankfurt

Private collection, Cologne

Private Collection, Portugal

Private Collection, Switzerland

POSSIBLE WORLDS : SULPTURE FROM EUROPE

9 November 1990 - 6 January 1991

The exhibition is a collaboration between the ICA and the Serpentine Gallery

Curated by Iwona Blazwick, James Lingwood and Andrea Schlieker

© ICA, Serpentine Gallery

Catalogue designed by Arefin and Arefin, London

Printed by EGA, Brighton
in an edition of 1500

ISBN 1 87081485 1
ISBN 0 905263 87 1

As an independent educational charity the Serpentine Gallery receives financial
support from the Arts Council of Great Britain and Westminster City Council. To
ensure the gallery is operational throughout the year, further income needs to be
generated from donations, covenants and sponsorship.

Serpentine Gallery
Kensington Gardens, London W2 3XA Tel: 071-402 6075

The Institute of Contemporary Arts is an independent educational charity and while
gratefully acknowledging the financial assistance of the Arts Council of Great
Britain, Westminster City Gouncil, the London Borough Grants Unit and the British
Film Institute, is primarily reliant on its box office income, membership and
donations.

ICA
The Mall, London SWIY 5AH Tel: 071-930 0493

cover:
detail from Thomas Schütte's *The Laundry* 1989

general note:
the varying specifications listed in the captions are determined by the particular
instructions given by each artist.